Managing People

Simon Birkenhead is a chief executive who has spent twenty-five years managing teams across early-stage technology start-ups to the very largest global organizations. He is recognized by his employees as an inspiring manager who is able to help them deliver their best work. Between 2014 and 2019 he didn't have a single employee resign from any of the businesses he led. Educated at Cambridge University and London Business School, Simon is a former global business leader at Google, where he led teams across four continents. He has also held business leadership positions at 3M, Telefónica and Gartner. Since becoming a CEO he has run a number of international businesses out of the UK and New Zealand. He is currently Chief Executive and Board Director for International Volunteer HQ, the world's largest volunteer travel company. *Managing People* is his first book.

Simon Birkenhead

Managing People

BUSINESS

PENGUIN BUSINESS EXPERTS

UK | USA | Canada | Ireland | Australia
India | New Zealand | South Africa

Penguin Business Experts is part of the Penguin Random
House group of companies whose addresses can
be found at global.penguinrandomhouse.com.

Penguin
Random House
UK

First published 2021
001

Text design by Richard Marston
Set in 11.75/14.75 pt Minion Pro
Typeset by Jouve (UK), Milton Keynes
Printed and bound in Great Britain by Clays Ltd,
Elcograf S.p.A.

The authorized representative in the EEA is
Penguin Random House Ireland, Morrison
Chambers, 32 Nassau Street, Dublin D02 YH68

A CIP catalogue record for this book is available
from the British Library

ISBN: 978–0–241–51346–0

Follow us on LinkedIn: https://www.linkedin.
com/company/penguin-connect/

www.greenpenguin.co.uk

MIX
Paper from
responsible sources
FSC® C018179

Penguin Random House is committed to a
sustainable future for our business, our readers
and our planet. This book is made from Forest
Stewardship Council® certified paper.

To all those who have suffered under a bad manager.
I hope this book will help others to avoid
similar experiences.

Contents

Contents

Introduction

Most managers fail. Some 70 per cent of employees say they are dissatisfied with their line manager. A shocking 50 per cent of managers are labelled as incompetent, a disappointment, a wrong hire or a complete failure by their co-workers.[1] Bad management is a leading cause of employees feeling unmotivated and underinspired. Stress, anxiety and mental-health problems in the workplace more often have less to do with the work people are asked to undertake than with the way they are managed, which is why disliking their boss is the number one reason people choose to leave their job.[2] Toxic work cultures are born out of incompetent management and act as a brake that holds back both individual performance and organizational success.

How is it that, 250 years after the Industrial Revolution, when the modern approach to management was born, most companies have still not worked out how to manage their employees effectively?

Most people are promoted because they are good at what they do, but becoming a manager is not a straightforward progression from a previous non-managerial position – rather, it is a move into an entirely new role, one that demands a set of skills, attitudes and behaviours very different from those you are used to. That's why a survey of 500 managers found 44 per cent felt unprepared for their role, with 87 per cent wishing they had received more training before becoming a manager.[3] In fact, most newly promoted managers (over 60 per cent in one study) are never given *any* formal training to prepare them for their new responsibilities.[4] They aren't told how to get the best performance from their employees, warned about the bad managerial habits that will alienate their team, or even informed of the basic expectations those they are managing will have of them.

Knowing how to manage people is not instinctive; you can't rely on your common sense. Given how many bad managers exist, you certainly shouldn't rely on emulating others. So, how can you avoid becoming one of those managers who destroy more value than they create? What should you do in order to become a great manager who is able to create exceptional performance from and satisfaction among your team?

Early in my career, I assumed all great managers had a natural talent. There seemed to be so few of them that I thought they must possess a magical ability to be brilliant at what they did, with unique personalities that made them perfectly suited for managing people effectively. Teams managed by these individuals exhibit less negativity and more genuine optimism and passion. Team chatter is focused on the positive activities they are engaging in rather than criticism of what isn't happening. Individuals try actively to find solutions rather than waiting expectantly for someone else to sort things out. Working long hours generates less stress and anxiety because team members are passionate about what they're doing. When things don't go to plan, the default reaction isn't to apportion blame (usually on the manager) but instead to examine what went wrong and find ways to avoid its repetition. In general, people in a well-managed team are happier and enjoy their jobs more than those who are badly managed.

I really wanted to be one of those managers, but doubted I could be. I was introverted yet arrogant, awkward around other people, lacked emotional intelligence and was overly dogmatic in my communication. But the more books, articles and research I read about how to get the best performance from others, the more I realized there was actually a set of disciplines I could follow that would help me achieve my goal. I discovered that, far from being an intrinsic talent awarded to only a select few, the skill of great people management could be acquired simply by learning a set of rules and applying them consistently. I had to unlearn some bad habits and actively adopt new behaviours that would overcome the drawbacks of my natural, default personality. As time went on, this new approach generated better relationships with my teams and my new behaviours became so natural that I no longer had to think about them. My communications softened, my emotional intelligence deepened and my new-found openness and authenticity generated more trust and respect.

I now know that anyone who is sufficiently motivated can become an inspiring manager by understanding and following the basic rules, frameworks and best practices I set out in this book. *Managing People* is a manual that will enable any first-time manager or established supervisor to succeed in their role by helping their team to be the best it can possibly be, and in the process become a manager others love working for. The majority of newly appointed managers have little idea what they need to do differently once they are given responsibility for someone else's performance. They have to learn on the job. This book offers both theoretical and practical measures that will help you to be effective from day one and avoid the experiential pitfalls many others fall into. By following my guidance, you'll be on your way to becoming the inspiring manager that your employees need if they are to succeed in their own careers.

The journey will take you from identifying the existing bad habits you need to leave behind through to the best practices you should adopt and the aspects of the job you must get right. Becoming a superstar manager is something that can be learnt and mastered, just like any other skill – you simply need to understand what to do and, most importantly, put in the practice. This book breaks down the task of people management into its core job responsibilities via a series of simple and easily followed guidelines.

Part 1: What Makes a Great Manager explains why your own ambition to become a highly effective manager is so important. You will learn how to avoid the most common mistakes that bad managers make, including the behaviours that demoralize their teams, create stress and destroy organizational culture. We'll then look at how the most capable managers are able to get the best out of their teams and will use these insights to build a framework you can use to become a highly effective manager yourself.

Part 2: The Five Steps to Being a Great Manager describes the five pillars of good leadership that you can use to get the best performance from your team: motivation, expectations, development, culture and communication. Each of the five chapters offers many practical suggestions to enable you to implement the best practices with confidence.

Part 3: Becoming the Manager You Aspire to Be draws everything together. With so many potential pitfalls, managing other people can seem overwhelming, so the book finishes with a handy summary of the best practices you'll have learnt, condensed into a list of the twenty most important things to get right as you embark on this next step in your professional career.

Before we begin, it is important to emphasize that knowledge has no value unless it is acted upon. The greatest success will come not from what you learn but from what you do. For this book to have a lasting positive impact on your career, and the careers of those you manage, you'll have to engage in some deep self-reflection that will allow you to identify those inbuilt attitudes that must change and the new, perhaps initially unnatural behaviours you will need to take on board. Managing people effectively is a challenge. It requires active, deliberate effort to tease out the best performance from your team.

Make a commitment to yourself now to make changes in how you operate as you work through this book. If you've done that, you're ready to start the journey to becoming the inspiring and supportive manager your employees want you to be.

Let's begin.

Part 1 What Makes a Great Manager?

Why Being a Great Manager Matters

Whether you are approaching a step up in your career or are an existing manager who wants to upskill and enhance your promotion prospects, one thing is for certain: your job as a manager will be very different from your past life as a team member. You'll have responsibilities that will impact not only the business you work for but also the lives of the people who work under you, their happiness and even their physical and mental well-being. You'll be pushed beyond most people's natural comfort zone and will have to deal with challenging and emotionally charged situations unlike any you've encountered before. Your team will judge everything you say and do, and even what you don't. Others will look to you for guidance, structure and feedback, and expect you to give it, regardless of whether you can or want to. And you'll have to do all this while keeping up with your other, non-supervisory work.

This all sounds terrifying, so it's understandable if you feel out of your depth and anxious. There's no denying that managing people can be very challenging at times, but it can also be hugely rewarding. Becoming a great manager grants you the satisfaction of seeing your employees develop and grow, helping them achieve things they never thought possible and getting the opportunity to deliver real benefits for your organization. All this will make up for any personal stress you might feel as you begin your journey. Over time, as you learn and improve, you'll come to love managing others.

My own career as a manager has followed this trajectory. I didn't enjoy managing at first because I wasn't sure what I was supposed to do. I made many mistakes because I didn't know any better. I was given my first few teams to manage with no guidance whatsoever as to what the new job entailed. I defaulted to what I thought was the right approach, but this relied on the assertion of my authority and I was wholly ignorant of the negative impact some of my behaviours were having on my team. Thankfully, I was given hard but valuable feedback. I'm someone who really hates not being the best at what I do, so once I was made aware that I was sometimes causing more harm than good, I vowed to learn how to become the best manager possible so that others would love working for me. I discovered an amazing feedback cycle: managing others in a more positive, motivating and collaborative way meant that they enjoyed their jobs more. The quality of their work improved, which meant they became easier to supervise, so I enjoyed my job more in turn. Because I was happier and more confident at work, I became a better leader, my team's performance improved, and the cycle continued. I'm now a CEO and I credit my own career success directly to the investment I have made over the last twenty years in learning how to master the job of managing others.

Managing People summarizes what I have discovered through fifteen years of research and putting the principles I've learnt into practice. If you know the core rules of managing people you will get the most important things right from day one, set the right personal ambitions and enable your on-the-job learning to be more focused and effective. By understanding the best-practice strategies and frameworks, you'll rely less on instinct and emulating the behaviours of your own (potentially mediocre) superiors and instead feel confident when faced with common managerial situations. By aspiring to be a manager that others *want* to work for, and not just someone they *have* to work for, you'll think less about what you want out of your employees and instead realize that managing people is all about understanding what *they* want from *you*. With practice and over time, you'll become a master at anything your team puts in front of you.

Why happiness drives success

We tend to view businesses according to the quality of the products or services they offer. But all organizations are really just a collection of people who follow processes and procedures. While it may be the appeal of their products that drives customer interest, every organization is reliant upon each employee doing their job effectively for its customers to be satisfied and for the business to succeed. It's people who design, promote and sell products. It's the frontline employees who build and maintain customer relationships. It's the warehouse staff who ensure deliveries arrive on time at the right destination. The processes and bureaucracy that determine how well – or not – things work in an organization are put in place by people. Imagine how much more successful your own company, or those you interact with, could be if everyone did their jobs effectively. No matter how superior your products or technologies might be, the success of every organization is underpinned by the effectiveness of its employees.

Employees are a critical driver of business success, and yet the quality of their effort largely comes down to one metric:

their happiness. Happy employees are far more effective, committed and productive than unhappy employees, as is shown by these two results from recent studies:

- Companies rated higher for employee satisfaction achieve between 10 and 16 per cent more profitability annually compared to those rated lower.[1]

- Workers make 13 per cent more sales in weeks where they report being happy compared to weeks when they are unhappy.[2]

Happy employees have been consistently shown to work harder, provide better customer service, develop stronger relationships and produce higher quality output; organizations with dissatisfied and unmotivated employees fail to achieve their potential because individuals are less effective and underutilized. After all, employee output is determined not by time worked but by how productive people are during the time they work and the quality of the effort they put in. Unhappy staff simply don't try so hard.

Britain's economic productivity growth over the decade 2010 to 2019 was the worst since the Industrial Revolution 250 years earlier.[3] Much of the blame for this is placed on the legacy of the 2008 financial crisis and a failure of British businesses to invest in technology, but the impact on output of an unhappy, unmotivated and poorly managed workforce cannot be ignored. Several studies in both the United States and the United Kingdom found that the average office worker is truly productive for only three to four hours a day. Gallup's *State of the Global Workplace* study found that across 142 countries, only 13 per cent of people say they are consistently fully engaged at work. Nearly one in five (19 per cent) claim they are 'actively disengaged' – meaning they are deliberately trying to put in as little effort as possible.[4] Many companies around the world have tried to improve employee engagement by experimenting with four-day working weeks and have discovered that output is actually higher than when employees were working five days a week because the greater flexibility boosts employee satisfaction and happier employees are more productive. Microsoft trialled a four-day work week in its Japanese offices in 2019 and found productivity grew by almost 40 per cent, despite a 20 per cent cut in hours.[5] Perpetual Guardian trialled a four-day work week in 2018 and also found employee engagement increased 40 per cent, leading it to make the policy permanent.[6]

If business performance is so closely aligned with employee satisfaction, then understanding why people choose to quit can help us identify the underlying causes of their unhappiness. An offer of a higher salary is rarely the true reason why people resign: just 12 per cent of employees leave their job because they want more money, despite 89 per cent of their managers believing this is why they quit.[7] Even when departing employees claim they are leaving for career advancement or more money, they are likely to have begun exploring other employment options because of frustrations or issues they have with their current job. Humans dislike change, so to contemplate changing your job, company, work location, even where you live, requires a significant push away from the current situation in addition to the potential lure of the new role.

While every individual's situation is different, people generally choose to leave a company for one or more of these three main reasons:

1 They don't feel motivated.

2 They feel that they aren't learning, developing or progressing.

3 They don't like their boss.

While only the third point directly relates to the behaviour of the manager, all three reasons fall within the manager's scope of responsibilities. Employees expect their manager to motivate them, support their personal development and establish a trust-based, respectful and supportive working relationship. The manager is at the heart of why most people choose to change jobs. How much you like your boss is the biggest single influence on your overall feeling of satisfaction at work.[8] All other factors relating to employee happiness are secondary to this.

As a manager, you will be the most important person in the company so far as your team is concerned. You have the ability to influence their motivation and enjoyment, their learning and development, their effectiveness and productivity, their schedule and workload. You'll control whom they work with, the work they're asked to do and the systems, culture and environment within which they have to operate. A great manager can turn a group of mediocre individuals into a high-performing team; conversely, a bad manager can take a team of top employees and implode their performance, causing the stars among them to flee and the remainder to descend into a black hole of stress, frustration and unhappiness. Above every employee who doesn't seem to care about their work there is usually a manager who doesn't care about them.

If you want to make the greatest possible contribution to your organization, then your highest priority must be to ensure that each person you manage is engaged and operating at maximum potential. Learning how to do this is what this book is all about.

....

Chapter takeaways

- Employee satisfaction is the greatest driver of company performance.

- The effectiveness of a manager and how they work with their team is the greatest driver of employee happiness at work.

- Becoming a great manager is something you can learn and master but requires conscious effort to achieve.

The Bad Habits You Must Break

If you're more than a few years into your career, you will almost certainly have experienced a bad manager at some point, perhaps even a terrible one. Is that what has motivated you to learn how to do a better job by reading this book? Understanding *why* these managers were ineffective is an essential first step in your own development journey. Becoming an exceptional manager is not only about adopting new ways of thinking and behaving; you'll also have to unlearn and shed some of your default behaviours that have helped you to perform well enough to warrant promotion to a managerial role. These will be so ingrained in how you operate that you might not even be aware of them. This chapter is all about helping you to develop deeper self-awareness of behaviours or attitudes that will prevent you becoming a strong manager. We'll do this by examining why so many mediocre managers exist, exploring how these individuals create stress, frustration, disappointment and wasted effort among their teams and asking whether you recognize any of these behaviours in yourself.

I've been working for twenty-six years. During this time, I have had twenty-one different managers across eleven companies. With a few exceptions, they have all given me valuable insights into how *not* to manage people. I've learnt more from the flaws in their management techniques because it's so much easier (and cathartic) as an employee to identify and criticize others' failures than to praise their strengths. My experience is not exceptional. Ask any of your friends about how they are managed at work and I'm sure they will share a long list of frustrations alleviated by remarkably few positives. While you might be relieved to hear that you're not alone in having been managed poorly, this is a shocking indictment of the quality of management in organizations today. That some 57 per cent of employees choose to quit their jobs because of their boss, with a further 32 per cent sticking around but dreaming of how they might get away,[1] indicates there are very few role models out there for you to learn from.

We're in this situation for two main reasons. Firstly, organizations generally promote people who are strong performers in their current role. But strong functional expertise in one role is no guarantee of success in managing others, especially since the skills, responsibilities and outcomes are vastly different. Partners in law firms have been elevated to the top of their organization through their legal expertise, but I've heard shocking stories about how some treat their juniors, which includes ignoring the very employment laws they advise their clients on every day. I've seen sales reps flee from a team when a high-performing peer is elevated to the team leader role because their new manager had always been so focused on their own performance that they had no idea how to help others achieve similar success. I have friends in HR reporting to senior managers who fail to live by the best practices they spend all day advising others on. These people haven't deliberately chosen to be bad managers; most simply fail to grasp the negative impact that they are having on others. Some even mistakenly assume that what they're doing is actually beneficial for their team, failing to realize that what made them so successful as an individual can be detrimental to their performance as a manager. Unfortunately, when these mediocre managers become senior executives, there's nobody at the top of the hierarchy advocating for better management because they don't see the gap between what's being accepted and what could be possible. A manager doesn't need to be the most technically capable person in the team. Indeed, a manager's technical skills have been shown to be among the least influential contributions to an employee's performance.[2] It is entirely possible for someone to become a very successful manager without having been the highest-performing employee. Unfortunately, these individuals are rarely given the opportunity to demonstrate this because they are frequently overlooked for promotion.

However, the second reason mediocre managers are so pervasive – and one that's more easily addressed – is that few of them received any formal training when they were first promoted. Nobody told them what it takes to motivate, guide and inspire others. Most don't even know this is something they're expected to do. Organizations assume that first-time managers will either somehow already know what to do or that they will be able to 'figure it out'. As I discovered early in my career, copying how others manage or relying upon supposed common sense, will rarely lead to success.

There's no need to assume or accept mediocrity. You shouldn't base your managerial benchmark on being not as bad as those around you. You mustn't strive to exceed only the low bar set by others. You should plan to be the high bar that others will then measure themselves against. By learning how to become a truly inspiring, effective and successful manager, you can avoid becoming one of the 60 per cent of newly promoted managers who are regarded as failures by their superiors or by those they manage.[3] If I can do it, you can too.

Bad bosses: the twenty worst managerial behaviours to avoid

Now that you understand why it is so important for you to become a great manager who is surrounded by a happy and productive team, and why you shouldn't copy the behaviours of other managers around you, I want to turn your attention inwards on to your own current default behaviours. Take an honest look at how you have got to where you are today. What attitudes and behaviours towards others have helped you so far, but may hinder you going forward? You can't progress to becoming a great manager until you acknowledge and address the barriers that will prevent you getting there.

The best way to do this is by exploring the most common characteristics of managers who are rated poorly by their employees and reflecting on whether any of these traits are applicable to you. I love the term 'accidental diminishers', coined by author Liz Wiseman, which describes managers who reduce the performance of those around them yet remain clueless about the negative impact they are having. Employees working under a diminishing manager only deliver between 20 per cent and 50 per cent of their total potential capability.[4] By openly acknowledging any diminishing attributes you may unwittingly exhibit now, you'll gain the self-awareness to consciously avoid continuing these habits as a manager.

Although every bad manager is different, there are twenty common attitudes and behaviours exhibited by managers who create the most frustration, stress and wasted effort in their teams. These fall roughly into three categories:

- **Persona:** The manager's workplace personality.

- **Operational:** How the boss chooses to work.

- **Expertise:** Their experience (or lack of it).

Persona

1 **Insensitive and uncaring:** Lack of interest in others, poor at handling matters in a sensitive manner, little appreciation of how others feel.

2 **Weak control over their own emotions:** Exhibits bursts of visible frustration, rage or tears.

3 **Dictatorial or tyrannical:** Behaving in an authoritarian manner that suppresses other people's ideas, using stress and anxiety as management tools.

4 **Bully:** Aggressive, confrontational or demeaning behaviour.

Operational

5 **Poor communicators:** Nobody knows what's going on, what decisions have been made or why something's important.

6 **Disorganized and unreliable:** Constantly firefighting, with tasks delegated at the last minute or simply forgotten.

7 **Indecisive:** Everybody's productivity declines as nothing is ever decided.

8 **Fails to deal with problems:** Everyone else can see what's wrong but the manager does nothing about it, blindly ignoring realities, especially the disruption that a poorly performing team member can cause.

9 **Poor delegation:** Not effectively explaining what they want done, creating wasted effort when the end result isn't what they had expected.

10 **Micro-management:** Failing to trust others to do what's needed, or simply telling them what to do in precise detail. (This trait is very common among newly appointed managers who regard themselves as a strong subject-matter expert.)

11 **Inconsistent, contradictory or unpredictable:** Frequently changes opinion on matters, causing work to be wasted.

12 **Quick to take over:** Jumps in and takes control when they see people struggling, but by doing so they prevent their team from developing.

13 **Ignores constraints:** Pushes their own agenda with little appreciation of other people's existing priorities, workload, commitments or capacity, creating stress when the work exceeds individuals' ability to deliver.

14 **Self-promoting politician:** Takes all the credit while delegating all the blame.

15 **Empire builder:** Only interested in acquiring and hoarding resources for their own ego and self-promotion, while underutilizing each employee.

Expertise

16 **Know-it-all:** Seemingly has the answers to everyone's problems so team members stop thinking for themselves.

17 No clear strategy: Great at stimulating ideas but with no clear vision for what everyone is trying to achieve or why, creating a tsunami of constantly changing priorities.

18 Inability to implement: Big thinkers who cast a compelling vision but have little grasp on the reality of how to actually deliver it.

19 Perfectionist: Leaders who strive for excellence and focus on the finest details to the detriment of the need to think about the bigger picture and move fast.

20 Poor job-specific expertise: Unable to direct, train, coach or assess the performance of team members because they don't know what each person should be doing.

Often more than one of the traits above are combined into a perfect storm of bad management.

CASE STUDIES

Nick has a boss who constantly leaves tasks to the last minute because she is hopelessly disorganized and indecisive, which creates stress and wasted effort in her team. Nick knows weeks in advance about most important client presentations, yet his manager usually doesn't provide him with guidance on what to prepare until a couple of days before each meeting, and then she doesn't offer feedback on what Nick has prepared until the evening before they're due to meet the client. This feedback then often contradicts the original guidance she gave Nick, requiring him to rewrite a lot of his work overnight. Nick's boss gets angry at his apparent incompetence, oblivious of how her own lack of foresight and strategy has created this situation. The stress caused by his manager's flip-flopping opinions and her insensitivity to his personal time means he's on the brink of quitting and finding another job.

Jennifer works for a law firm. Her manager seems to believe that people perform best when under stress. He delegates by shouting instructions, setting entirely unrealistic and unreasonable deadlines and expecting Jennifer to work through her weekends to get her tasks done. She's at breaking point and has had enough. Her manager is extremely smart and competent in his functional role but appalling to work for. Everyone who works for or with him knows this, but nobody in the firm's upper management will do anything about his management practices because he generates enormous revenue through his client relationships. Jennifer's story is a great example of how so many organizations have fallen into the trap of failing to deal with bad managers for fear of upsetting the revenue stream they generate.

Stories I've heard about bad managers make it clear that people have the least patience for managers who create wasted work or unnecessarily encroach on personal time through their own incompetence and lack of consideration for others. People want to know that their efforts have an impact. That's why our motivation can be destroyed through work that's wasted owing to unclear instructions or repeated changes of opinion. People hate losing control of their own time, so having to work late or at weekends because of someone else's failures can create real resentment. Managers who are disorganized, inconsistent, indecisive or poor delegators can create the most stress and disillusionment of all. There are millions of other Nicks and

Jennifers who are one late night away from throwing in the towel and taking their talents elsewhere.

You may have your own examples of bad managerial behaviours from those you have worked for or alongside in the past. Take a moment now to appreciate what these managers did that angered, upset or stressed you. Viewing all these traits through the eyes of the recipient may give you an alternative perspective on your own managerial behaviours. Be completely honest with yourself about whether you exhibit any of the bad habits described above, consciously or otherwise.

Acknowledging your own bad habits

Developing self-awareness is an important first step in becoming a better manager. To be successful in your ambitions, you must make an honest assessment of how you work with others. If you don't, you'll risk becoming an accidental diminisher who assumes the skills, experience and behaviours that have got you to where you are will continue to carry you through. Most new managers need to shed at least a few of the default behaviours that made them excellent individual contributors, so please take a moment to reflect on any you may need to adapt.

Which three of the twenty traits listed above are most likely to be your worst blind spots? If you're unsure, then perhaps you've never been given feedback on *how* you work. If so, then now is the ideal time to ask for it. By explaining to your co-workers, customers or supervisors that you wish to develop your self-awareness in order to assist your transition into a managerial position, you'll create a safe space for them to offer you honest feedback on their experience of working with you. To build a fully rounded picture of how others perceive you, I suggest you ask for their opinion (to be offered anonymously, if you think it would provide more frankness) on how they rate you in these areas:

- **Emotional intelligence:** Your ability to understand how others are feeling and to express yourself in ways that are sensitive to others.

- **Consideration:** How open you appear to the opinions, ideas and circumstances of others.

- **Appreciation:** Whether others feel you show appreciation for their work.

- **Communication:** How effective you are at listening, explaining and influencing.

- **Organization:** How well you manage yourself and others.

- **Decisiveness:** Your ability and willingness to make decisions and how likely you are to then change your mind.

- **Management style:** How effectively you delegate and guide others (whether or not you are actually a manager).

- **Strategic vision:** Whether you appear to be guided by a clear understanding of what you and your co-workers need to do and why.

- **Supervisory skills:** How well others feel you support them and their work.

For a sample questionnaire you can use to solicit feedback from others, visit www.managingpeople.tips.

Don't assume behaviours are ingrained into your personality

and are 'just the way you are'. Considerable psychological research has revealed our personalities are fluid and can be shaped through conscious effort that redirects our subconscious habits. I have become more extrovert, emotionally intelligent, sensitive and authentic simply through self-awareness, motivation, effort and practice. If you put your mind to it, you can mould your persona to shed bad default behaviours that will hold you back and adopt the new best-practice approaches detailed in the remainder of this book.

As a manager, it's not your own knowledge that will make you a success, but rather your interpersonal and communication skills, combined with your ability to motivate and coordinate the work of others. Managing people is not about how much you know but how well you tap into how much other people know. From this point on, we're going to focus on what you *should* do, rather than what you shouldn't.

Chapter takeaways

- The skills required to be an effective manager are different from those that got you promoted. Don't assume that the behaviours and attitudes that made you a strong individual performer will make you a highly effective manager.

- Most mediocre managers exhibit a similar set of diminishing behaviours. Self-awareness will help you to shed any of these that will hold you back as a manager.

What Your Employees Need from You

Now that we have covered the behaviours common to people no one likes working for, let's turn our attention to the ways of working you *should* adopt in order to become a great manager who is able to inspire others to achieve their best.

Many of the performance-diminishing behaviours covered in the last chapter stem from a mistake common to many ineffective managers: the assumption that 'managing' means 'getting others to do what you want'. In fact, the opposite is true: mastering people management is about appreciating and acting on what your employees want and expect from *you*.

Of course, managers are tasked with ensuring their reports deliver the work that the team or organization requires, but, as noted in the first chapter, the greatest contributor to company performance is employee satisfaction. The best managers see themselves as working for their team to ensure each member is both able and willing to perform at their best. An orchestra's conductor plays no instrument, yet without him or her its musical output would be unsynchronized. The conductor works for the orchestra, not the other way round. Our focus for this chapter is how you, as a manager, can build an engaged and satisfied team whose members are motivated to produce great work. What can and should you do to create and sustain such high levels of employee satisfaction?

Project Oxygen

In 2008 Google launched Project Oxygen, an initiative that aimed to identify what makes a great manager by discovering how the managers of Google's most effective teams worked and whether there were any common practices that could be implemented across the company to raise other teams' performance. Employee satisfaction was taken as the measure of how well each manager operated, with individual appraisal ratings and team contribution used to categorize how well each team was performing.

The project concluded that there were ten managerial behaviours that were highly correlated with team performance. In other words, the scores a manager received on these ten behaviours were predictors of how well their team would perform. The higher the manager was rated on this behavioural scale, the better their team's outcomes were over the subsequent year. Each team member was also more likely to claim higher satisfaction at work and be regarded as a better individual performer. The ten behaviours were, in order of importance:

1 Is a good coach.

2 Empowers their team and avoids micro-managing.

3 Creates an inclusive environment for their team, showing concern for their success and well-being.

4 Is productive and results orientated.

5 Is a good communicator who listens to their team and shares information.

6 Supports career development and discusses performance.

7 Sets a clear and consistent vision and strategy for the team.

8 Has strong job-specific technical skills to help advise the team.

9 Collaborates across the organization.

10 Is a strong decision-maker.

While role-specific technical expertise is clearly important for a manager to be able to coach, direct and assess individual team members, it is worth recognizing that this requirement features low down on Google's list – it is among the least influential factors. This reaffirms that the talents and experience you have as a strong individual contributor do not necessarily translate to you being an effective manager. Managing people is not about what you know; it is about how well you access what other people know.[1]

Project Oxygen is just one of dozens of studies I've reviewed that have tried to identify the secrets behind great managers' performance. While the terminology is different in each study, I discovered a consistency in the underlying managerial responsibilities they listed. I saw that every set of six or ten or twelve core behaviours identified by each study could be summarized by just five fundamental responsibilities that drive almost all of the impact managers have on employees. These five pillars are what underpin the most effective managers. I'm confident that anyone can become an effective manager by understanding each one, its importance, how to use it and how it works in tandem with the others. Think of them as your tickets to managerial success.

The five pillars of successful people management

Despite 70 per cent of employees saying they are unhappy with the way they are managed, the job of being a people manager is remarkably straightforward. Like any other job, you just need to understand and follow the job description. Unfortunately, most managers simply don't know what that job description is because nobody has told them. Before researching and writing this book, I had never imagined the job of managing others could be summarized by a simple list of just five core tasks. Yet my research and experience have shown that it can.

Here are the five pillars of effective people management that should form your job description if you want to be regarded as a great manager by those you're responsible for:

1 **Motivation:** Keeping your employees engaged in their job, with the drive and desire to do the best work they can.

2 **Expectations:** Ensuring each employee knows their objectives and what is expected of them, as well as holding them accountable for delivering these.

3 **Development:** Providing training, coaching and support to your employees to equip them with what they need to succeed.

4 **Culture:** Creating a productive and inclusive working environment that enables and encourages everyone to work at their highest level at all times.

5 **Communication:** Ensuring there is clear and consistent two-way communication so that messages are understood and actioned.

If you focus on these five pillars and execute them consistently, you will provide your people with everything they need to perform at their peak. While the list might read like a series of common-sense approaches, the fact that so many mediocre managers exist demonstrates that few actually put them into practice.

Employees instinctively look for support in all these areas. We have already seen that people generally decide to quit a job when either they don't feel motivated, they aren't learning, developing or progressing, or they don't have a positive relationship with their boss. Most people need a little encouragement; they want to understand what's expected of them, feel supported and be able to work in a pleasant environment. Managers who fail to take responsibility for one or more of these pillars create frustrated employees and sub-optimal performances.

Has a manager ever given you responsibility for a project without clearly explaining in detail what they expected you to do or why it was important? Have you ever been part of a toxic culture that held you back because you didn't feel supported or couldn't trust others? Has there been a time when you have been given a task but felt ill-equipped to do it as well as you wanted because you simply didn't have the skills or knowledge? Situations such as these can create deep anxiety when, despite someone's wish to do a good job, they are prevented from doing so by a manager who is not fulfilling their responsibilities and executing all five pillars of good management.

Average managers – in other words, the majority of them – pay lip-service to these tasks. They fail to appreciate all that they must do under each pillar for them to excel in their roles. The five chapters in Part 2 address these pillars in turn. Each provides a detailed explanation of exactly what's involved, along with practical recommendations that will allow you to be highly effective from day one. Master each of these and you'll become the successful manager that you aspire to be.

....

Chapter takeaways

The job description for your role as a people manager comprises five pillars of responsibility that you should use to derive the best performance from your employees:

- Motivation.
- Expectations.
- Development.
- Culture.
- Communication.

Part 2 The Five Steps to Being a Great Manager

Step 1: Activate Motivation

Why we work

Everything we do, and everything we choose not to do, is driven by our motivations. These are the forces that make us go to work, put effort into our tasks and set aside time for things that interest us. They are also the forces that encourage us to call in sick when we just want a day off, make us put only half-hearted effort into a project and create sufficient disengagement for us to decide to quit our jobs. Unless you appreciate why people work, you'll never be able to achieve your desired impact or extract the maximum potential from others. In our modern workplace, you can't just tell someone to do a better job and expect that they will. They must want to give their best efforts willingly, and you must be their inspiration. That's why the first pillar of great management is motivation.

Formal and informal authority

Bad managers are often entirely ignorant of the fact that their employees need to be motivated. In the absence of motivation as a management tool, they rely on hierarchical leadership, where senior managers wield power by cascading instructions down from above. This style of management dates from the Industrial Revolution, when the modern-day organization was born. In factories with monotonous, repetitive jobs, managers didn't want employees to question their direction. Getting paid was seen as sufficient motivation for people to do their work. Today, we describe this type of management style as using *formal authority* to get work done.

Formal authority derives from the hierarchy of a typical organization. You are expected to do what those higher up tell you to do, unquestioningly, because you work for them. They make the decisions, they assess your performance, they control how much you're paid and they decide whether you get promoted or fired. Formal authority is primarily about power, obedience and compliance.

Formal authority is the lazy way to manage. It's easy to give a subordinate a task and expect them to do it if not doing so carries the fear of a bad appraisal or even dismissal as the consequence. But this doesn't mean the employee will do the job well. In today's knowledge-based economies, where the talents and tasks of individual employees vary and a company's success is determined by how well those talents are harnessed and put to good use, it's clear that reliance upon formal authority is outdated and ineffective. Raising performance to a higher level requires more than delegating diktats.

Jennifer, whom we met earlier, is an example of someone being managed through formal authority. Her manager does nothing to make her want to deliver good work. He relies upon a stick rather than a carrot, shouts rather than encourages and issues task commands rather than problems to solve. There's little encouragement or gratitude, and she receives feedback only when her boss isn't happy with what she's produced. Any manager who has used the phrase 'Do A or else suffer B' is relying upon formal authority and their hierarchical position to get a job done.

A much more effective way to lead people is through *informal authority*, which is created through interpersonal connections that are built up over time through four factors:

- **Trust:** 'I believe what you say.'

- **Respect:** 'I admire your past achievements.'

- **Relationship:** 'I like you as a person.'

- **Knowledge and experience:** 'I believe you are best placed to make this decision.'

While your formal authority makes others work because they have to, your informal authority encourages others to work because of the relationship they have with you. Weak managers, especially newly appointed ones, tend to depend on the power derived from their position because their informal authority proves insufficient. It's one reason why a recent study by global talent business ADP found that just 16 per cent of people feel fully engaged with their work. The other 84 per cent haven't been given a strong reason to *want* to work hard.[1] Why we work determines how well we work, and both are driven by what we're motivated to do.

What drives our motivation?

As a manager, motivation is the most powerful weapon in your armoury. When someone isn't motivated, it feels as though you are pushing a huge rock up a hill. It's hard to make progress and as soon as you stop pushing, momentum stalls. But when that same employee does get behind something, voluntarily putting in the effort that's needed to achieve the objective, the gradient of the hill reverses and the rock tumbles down on its own, building momentum as it goes, with little extra effort required on your part to sustain its progress.

To understand how you can harness your employees' motivation as a manager requires appreciation of the important differences between two forms of motivation: intrinsic and extrinsic.

Intrinsic motivation derives from something inside you, an emotional drive that's an essential component of your own interests, goals, sense of self and personality. It's what makes you want to do things. We each experience intrinsic motivation through our unique interests and ambitions. I'm motivated by a sense of personal achievement and creativity, so I'm willing to spend my weekends writing because I enjoy the thought process and it gives me a deep sense of fulfilment and satisfaction. It's also why I enjoy photography, growing businesses and becoming involved in projects where I can see the impact of my contributions. You can identify your own intrinsic motivations by thinking about the activities you actively choose to spend your time doing in your work and personal life. What do you readily undertake without hesitation and with a sense of excitement? What activities at work are you willing to stay late to finish off even when you don't have to? What do you look forward to doing at the weekends? If you won the lottery and could give up work, what would you choose to do with your time?

We find it much harder to motivate ourselves to do things we don't enjoy, such as homework, filling in our tax returns or maintaining a strict diet. In these circumstances, we usually need to rely on external motivators to force us into doing these activities, such as the social group that encourages us to stick with the diet, the personal trainer who ensures we attend our weekly gym session, the threat of a fine if our tax return is late, or the nagging parent who makes their child complete their schoolwork. These are *extrinsic motivations* because they derive from someone or something encouraging, pressuring or rewarding us.

Intrinsic motivation is generally positive in nature because it is tied directly to what we want to do – our *desires*. In a work context, it improves performance effortlessly: we're self-motivated to do work we enjoy or get satisfaction from. Therefore, as a manager, this is something you should try hard to activate in your employees.

Extrinsic motivation, in contrast, is about *pressure* and *compliance* – what someone else wants us to do, not what we want to do ourselves. Extrinsic motivations come from the expectations and demands placed on us by our manager, our team, our family or the broader society we inhabit. Peer pressure, annual bonuses, penalties and social norms are all examples of extrinsic motivations because they pressure us to behave unnaturally.

The differences in how organizations view these two types of motivation were highlighted during the Covid-19 pandemic of 2020/21, when large portions of the global workforce were required to work from home when their countries went into lockdown. For many organizations, it seemed management's highest priority was to figure out how they could use technology to check whether their remote employees were actually working, rather than considering how they could keep their employees engaged and motivated during the crisis.

When we think about what we're self-motivated by at work – what drives our intrinsic motivation – almost everything that pushes us positively forward falls into one of three motivational categories:

- **Play:** We work because we enjoy it. Whether it is the intellectual stimulation, learning experience or just simply the fun we have while doing it, our work is something we voluntarily want to do for the sheer joy of it. The activity itself is the reward.

- **Potential:** We work because it will help us progress towards a future goal. We might want to have a certain job title, learn new skills, or simply strive for the satisfaction that comes from completing a project, and we work to achieve that end result.

- **Purpose:** We work because the impact we deliver is important to us. Our altruistic personality places a high value on the wider benefit our work delivers for others and that, in itself, provides us with the motivation to do the work.

If someone says they love what they do – they are being driven by the *Play* motive. It may not even be the actual work or activity itself that creates this pleasure; it could simply come from the colleagues they work with or just the environment they work in. The important thing is they enjoy what they do, and that's sufficient to motivate them to continue doing it every day.

Law firms and management consultancies rely heavily on the *Potential* motive by dangling the opportunity of becoming a partner in the business to encourage their junior employees to work hard and remain loyal. Despite having to work long hours and endure considerable stress, many perceive the dream of making partner sufficient to motivate them to stick with it.

People are motivated by *Purpose* when they find satisfaction in doing something for somebody else. Charities and not-for-profit organizations are able to attract and retain talented employees, despite generally offering salaries below those attainable elsewhere, because those individuals are motivated by the cause they are supporting. They are willing to sacrifice some of their own potential income in order to reap the personal rewards that come from contributing positively to their wider society.

Take a moment now to think about how your choices in your own social and work life are influenced by these three forces. For example, what has driven you to read this book?

- Do you simply enjoy reading business books and this one seemed interesting? (*Play*)

- Do you have an ambition to progress in your chosen career and you've realized that mastering your people management skills will support this? (*Potential*)

- Do you want to help the individuals in your team thrive and achieve their full potential? (*Purpose*)

If you're motivated by a combination of two or all three forces, then you should be really fired up to achieve great things. On the other hand, if you're reading this book simply because someone else told you to, then you're being extrinsically motivated. Perhaps you should consider why you lack an intrinsic desire to learn more about management. After all, if you don't have the self-motivation to read this book, will you be motivated to act on it and become a better manager for your team?

Extrinsic motivations are much weaker than their intrinsic counterparts and can have a negative effect on performance because they are exerted on us from outside. These are the forces that formal authority unleashes. We feel the need to comply either because that's how others expect us to behave or because we need something and this is the only way to get it. The extrinsic forces that power us have little to do with what we would actually choose to do and more with what we feel pressured to do, which is why they are less effective at delivering superior performance. I label extrinsic forces as negative motivators not because the motivation is necessarily bad but because they pressure you to do something you may not otherwise choose to do.

Negative motivations can be caused by:

- **Emotional pressure:** You work because some external force is threatening your identity. This might be guilt, fear, peer pressure or simply a desire to avoid disappointing someone else. Your motivation is driven by what you feel obliged to achieve – such as living up to others' expectations of you – rather than the work itself.

- **Economic pressure:** You work to achieve the reward on offer (your salary, a bonus or a prize) or to avoid a punishment (such as a fine or threat of losing your job), and not because you're motivated by the work.

- **Inertia:** You work for no real reason other than habit or an aversion to change. Most people stick with what they have unless there is a very good reason to switch, even sometimes *despite* there being a good reason to switch. Economists William Samuelson and Richard Zeckhauser have dubbed this behaviour 'status quo bias',[2] and it is the main headwind you'll face as a manager when trying to drive change in your team.

Most of us live with economic pressure: we need our income to maintain the lifestyle we're used to or achieve the lifestyle we desire. This pressure acts as a greater force for some, a lesser force for others. Many jobs with extremely high levels of stress and personal sacrifice (such as an expectation to work weekends or travel away from home for long periods) often have to compensate for a lack of intrinsic motivation by offering outsized salaries to retain employees. The lifestyle that these salaries enable then creates an economic force: these individuals don't want to give up the large houses and expensive holidays that their salaries support, so they feel forced to continue working, often in jobs they no longer enjoy. Those in lower-paid professions are especially impacted by economic forces because budgets are so constrained, but other intrinsic motivations can keep these people from pursuing higher-paid jobs that are less enjoyable. For example, the personal intrinsic rewards from nursing (Play and Purpose motives) can counterbalance the desire to earn more money.

Motivational forces are not binary: they all act on us constantly, though to differing levels. The best managers find ways to maximize their employees' intrinsic (positive) motivations, without relying upon extrinsic (negative) motivations. When we're highly motivated, we're happy and full of energy. Play, Potential and Purpose all help to create engaged employees. emotional and economic pressure and inertia all contribute towards stress, worry, self-doubt or disengagement. Companies whose cultures maximize intrinsic motivations while minimizing the extrinsic ones are most likely to produce superior business outcomes.

How to motivate through Play

While few jobs realistically offer the opportunity to 'play' at work, we all have a desire to enjoy what we do. So, how can you as a manager develop Play as a motivational force for your employees?

Dissatisfaction is a major barrier to motivation, but you don't always need to make people satisfied to remove it – you just need to get rid of the sources of their dissatisfaction. When people say they are stressed out at work, it is most often due to a loss of control over what they are tasked with doing or the schedule in which they must do it. Because we rarely choose to do things we don't enjoy, offering individuals greater choice over what they do, how they do it and their work schedule is a highly effective way to activate their Play motivation. After all, if you had hired Michelangelo to paint the Sistine Chapel, you wouldn't have told him how to hold his brush. Your employees were hired because of their talents. Your job as a manager is to define the *what*, not the *how*: assign goals then get out of the way so your employees can actually apply their skills and experience. By providing your team with autonomy, you'll enable those doing the work to determine how best to do it. When people are allowed to choose their tasks, processes and timetable, they will naturally elect to do them in ways that provide the most enjoyment and engagement and/or the least discomfort. This is Play in the context of the workplace.

The best way to provide autonomy to your team is to set expectations around outputs, not inputs. State clearly the results you expect your team to deliver but let them figure out how best to achieve them. I see so many job descriptions that describe in detail how someone is expected to do their job, but this assumes the writer of the job description knows more about the job than the person actually tasked with doing it. Managers rarely have the technical skills to be a master at doing each employee's job. Giving each person freedom to work the way they want to will allow them to enjoy the job more, and they are more likely to achieve superior results by applying their own knowledge and expertise in ways that might differ from your own assumptions.

Here are some other ways you can stimulate Play motivational forces in your team:

Bust bureaucracy

Often described as a tax on human achievement, bureaucracy was notably referred to by Jamie Dimon, CEO of JPMorgan Chase, as 'a disease that drives out good people'.[3] Left to their own devices, rules and processes can take on a life of their own, without regard to the actual value they deliver to the organization. Nobody enjoys fighting against the system to get anything done. When I worked at Google, we ran regular 'Bureaucracy Busters' – opportunities for employees to nominate time-wasting processes for review and elimination. Try identifying bureaucracy pressure points that hold your team back – then commit to fixing these. Every time an employee complains about a process or tool that's wasted their time, ask yourself why it is needed.

Get to know your team

The greatest Play motivation comes from the sheer pleasure of doing work you find immensely satisfying. Ask each member of your team, 'What have you enjoyed the most over the last couple of weeks?' or 'What's been your highlight of the week?' Try observing what each person spends more time on than might actually be necessary – chances are, they're putting more time in because they are enjoying the assignment. Then find ways to allow them to do more of this work in their role.

Assign challenges that make people think. The highest-performing individuals are often intellectually curious – they enjoy solving problems and won't give up until they've found a satisfactory answer. Setting them assignments that require creativity and thought will stimulate the enjoyment that comes from mastering a complex challenge.

Turn requests into questions. In place of saying 'This is what I want you to do', instead ask 'How would you approach this?' and empower the employee to solve the problem the way they think best.

Be flexible

The Covid-19 global pandemic showed us that flexible working arrangements can often function well if supported effectively by managers. Many companies, including Twitter and Unilever, have decided to let their employees work from home indefinitely for at least some of the week if they want to, with Unilever CEO Alan Jope admitting the five-day in-office structure they had pre-pandemic 'seems very old fashioned now'.[4] Some 90 per cent of employees claim that flexible work arrangements and schedules increase their morale because 9–5 simply doesn't work for every employee.[5] Flexibility supports autonomy – allowing people to work where and when they want. You can help your employees work at their best by finding the best schedule that works for them.

Embrace failure

Organizations go to great lengths to avoid failures, but experimentation and innovation stimulate interest, especially for higher-performing individuals who are rarely content with the status quo. People also learn more from their mistakes than their successes. Many start-ups adopt the philosophy of 'fail early and often' in order to fast-track their learning. Ed Catmull, president of Pixar Animation Studios, believes that 'If you aren't experiencing failure, then you are making a far worse mistake: You are being driven by the desire to avoid it.'[6] The desire for guaranteed success encourages the minimization of risk over exploration of potential. Rather than focusing time and effort on preventing failures, allow your team to move fast and try new things – but ensure everyone learns from ideas that don't work out so that they aren't repeated. Welcome mistakes as a consequence of innovation.

Introduce some 'play' time

Several of the world's most innovative companies, including Google and 3M, have famously allowed their engineers to spend a day a week on a personal side project that was tangential or unrelated to their core job. Some of Google's best-known products, such as Gmail and Google Maps, were born this way. Allowing your employees to work on their own personal-interest projects can provide a breath of fresh air and may lead them to fix something in the business that nobody else has spotted. I had one employee in a customer service role who was interested in learning more about marketing, so I asked her to critique our marketing emails. She came up with some terrific improvements through her experience of interacting with customers on a daily basis.

How to encourage ambition through Potential

Personal development gives us an inner energy because we see ourselves progressing to become something better – a faster runner, a better father, a more qualified accountant. The more progress we make towards our goal, the more motivated we become, and we lose interest quickly if the goal proves to be unattainable. The urge to become more competent in what we do and achieve an objective we feel passionate about has proved to be one of the best predictors of higher effort and productivity.

Video game designers understand better than most how learning and development create engagement. Games need to be addictive to make money for their designers, but any game quickly becomes boring if it doesn't challenge the player. In gaming, it's learning and progression that fuel our addiction. This is why the most successful games incorporate buckets of Potential motivation through leader boards, progression through increasingly challenging levels, the unlocking of rewards as tasks are completed and the mastering of skills, knowledge and tools. However, there's a delicate balance – make progression too difficult and the player may simply give up. As a manager, you can tap into this same motivational force by stimulating people's innate desire to develop and advance.

Most of us feel we have the potential to be better than we currently are, but not everyone has a clear ambition, and even fewer do something to actually achieve it. Those who say they have no real interest in self-improvement or progression feel that way simply because they aren't motivated by it. So, as a manager, you may need to stimulate that motivation by helping your employees understand what their potential is and where this could take them, and by mapping out a path that will get them there. Here are some tips on how you can do this:

Identify each of your team's personal development goals

If you don't know what an individual's learning goals are, you can't use these to motivate his or her work. Asking questions like 'What do you want to learn over the next few months?' and 'What would you like to be doing in a year's time?' can encourage them to think proactively about their own personal growth goals.

Actively support their ambitions

If someone can articulate what they want to achieve, help them to figure out how you, or the wider organization, can further that aim. If someone really wants a promotion, explaining to them where they are currently falling short of what's required will highlight how you could help them to develop additional experience in these areas – for example, by giving them more responsibility.

Help them see their potential

I once had a talented employee who didn't seem at all interested in career progression because the limited scope of her current role meant that she simply wasn't aware of other job options. She couldn't articulate her ambition because she didn't know what other opportunities there might be for her. You can help map out a potential future in such cases by facilitating a discussion around what interests them and therefore what other roles they might enjoy and do well in.

Give people bigger, juicier problems to solve

Easy tasks provide little motivation because they don't offer any opportunity to learn or improve. People feel more motivated when they are challenged, especially with big, significant problems that require more than just incremental improvements. That's why 'stretch' goals drive superior performance better than 'achievable' objectives as they encourage your employees to push themselves that bit harder.

Find each employee's 'native genius'

It's much easier to become better at something you already have a strong capability for. However, few of us actually realize what we're really good at because these tasks seem easy to us and so we don't appreciate that other people find them difficult. I've had employees who were so well organized that others were left in awe, but they didn't fully appreciate their unique talent because it's just the way they are. I call this a person's *native genius* – those talents that really set an individual apart. Figure out what these are for each of your employees, and then actually tell them. The knowledge that these skills are admired by others should stimulate further motivation to become even better at them.

Build self-belief

You can convince others that their ambition is achievable by addressing the mental constraints that create self-doubt and limit their thinking. By breaking down a stretch goal into smaller, more defined steps, you can help your employees to visualize a more achievable path that will get them to their destination.

Help fill in the gaps

Being asked to do work that exceeds a person's capabilities creates anxiety; being asked to do work that's too easy creates boredom. When you're setting expectations for your team, check that what you're asking for aligns with the skills and experience they offer. If there's a large competency gap, you risk creating a stressed-out employee. Instead of hoping the employee will 'figure things out', build a plan to help them develop the expertise needed to do the job well. I might ask the question, 'If I were to ask you to do this, how confident are you that you could do it well?' If the employee is honest in acknowledging their insecurities, you can scope out a personal development plan with them. If their self-confidence doesn't match reality, then this is a good time to make them aware of this.

Celebrate progress

Seeing progress towards a goal you care about is highly motivating. Celebrate small steps your team makes towards the goals you have set through team-wide announcements, celebratory drinks or even just a simple progress chart.

How to use impact to motivate through Purpose

Showing an employee or team how their work has meaning and contributes towards a larger goal – for themselves, the organization, or society at large – can be an immensely powerful way to stimulate intrinsic motivation. It's why people volunteer at soup kitchens for the homeless or help clear up a town after a storm. Working hard for something we don't care about creates apathy, but we become passionate when doing something that has real meaning for us. Without passion, a task is simply a chore. With passion, our work has purpose.

You can fire up your employees' Purpose motivational force through storytelling: explaining to people *why* their work matters. This is straightforward when your organization already has a clear altruistic purpose. At socially conscious outdoor company Patagonia everything evolves around its mission statement: 'We're in business to save our planet.' It is visible through its policy of recycling the clothes it sells, the messages it posts on social media and, for example, having on-site childcare at its head office. The company finances campaigns to elect politicians who support conservation, and recently donated its entire Black Friday sales in the US directly to environmental organizations. These purpose-led stories create a strong sense of belonging for both its employees and its customers.

Patagonia may be an extreme example, but motivation through purpose is possible in any company, even those with low-interest jobs that are highly repetitive and monotonous, such as in a factory, warehouse or shop. If a job is inherently uninteresting, it can still be made more meaningful by offering a rationale for why it's important the task is performed well. This can go a long way towards encouraging greater effort. If you're managing a box packer, you could explain to them why it is important they pack the boxes in a certain way: paint a picture of the excitement a customer has when receiving the item they've bought, and the disappointment they experience when they realize it has been damaged in transit. If you explain to the service staff in your restaurant why customer satisfaction is so important, they may appreciate how it could get them more tips. The famous anecdote about the janitor at NASA who was asked what he did in the organization and answered, 'I help put people on the moon,' may be apocryphal, but you get the point. The job may remain mechanical, but if you can create passion then at least those individuals might be more motivated to do it well.

Rallying troops behind a common goal is a sign of great leadership and that's exactly what you'll need to do to fire up your team's motivation through purpose. Here's how you can do this:

Explain why each person's job is important

The simple task of ensuring each team member fully appreciates *why* it is so important they do their job well can stimulate greater effort. What is the team trying to do and whom does it help? How are other people impacted if the employee does a great job, or a poor one? How does each individual's work materially contribute towards the wider objectives of the organization and its customers? For example, your receptionist contributes to the success of your company by creating a positive first impression for customers when they arrive.

Delegate with explanations

When assigning work, always explain why that particular activity is important to you, to the employee or to others. I've found one of the most powerful words in English is *because*, because the words that follow always provide an explanation. 'Please can you do this, because . . .' carries far more weight than just 'Please can you do this?' It will also help you avoid the most frequent response given when people are asked why they are doing something: 'Because the boss asked for it.' This is an extrinsic motivator that relies upon emotional pressure and formal authority, which is why few people are motivated by it.

Celebrate the impact

When a project or task is completed, it's so easy to tick it off your to-do list and move on to the next item. Before you forget what's been achieved, take a moment with your team to acknowledge – even celebrate – the impact of their last initiative. Ensure everyone appreciates that all their hard work made a difference to someone else, whether that's a customer, other colleagues or just the organization as a whole. Monthly team or company meetings are a terrific opportunity to celebrate successes and showcase what your team has delivered and the impact it has had. People quickly forget the hard work or difficult moments once they're overwhelmed by a sense of real achievement.

Ensure everyone hears from a real customer

Sharing customer stories about how your product or service has delivered real-life impact has been repeatedly shown to increase motivation. Charities invite the beneficiaries of their work to appear at fundraising events so that donors and fundraising employees hear real-life stories of the impact their contributions have made to people's lives. My current company has a dedicated channel on Slack called *#actuallynailedit* where we post positive feedback we receive from our customers or the latest five-star review on Trustpilot. If you run a sales team, you could ask each rep to share their best customer-success story in your weekly team meetings. Even if you don't run a customer-facing team, try to ensure that every one of your employees meets a real customer in person. When your team or organization hears at first-hand how customers value their work it can bring to life the importance of the job that they do.

Discover what motivates each person

We're all motivated by different things. Find out how each employee gains satisfaction in their job simply by asking them. Are they motivated by helping their customers, by supporting colleagues or by the work the organization does in the wider community?

Motivation quick wins: recognition and praise

Many of the suggestions above centre around what you do pre-task: motivating someone to do something before they have done it. But you can also deliver a big boost to motivation post-task. There are two easy ways to do this that will deliver speedy results: recognition and praise.

Underpinning all three drivers of intrinsic motivation is a desire to know you're doing a good job, that you're making an impact, and that this impact has been recognized by others. Recognizing an employee's good work – by letting them know you've noticed what they've done and appreciate it – is a really simple but highly effective way of firing up their motivation. Providing praise on top of this lets them know you think they've done their work exceptionally well. Both recognition and praise are free to give, can be offered both publicly and in private and can be repeated indefinitely provided they remain specific, sincere and genuine.

When offering praise, I follow a philosophy that has its origins in child psychology: I try to offer it when it is unexpected (so that it isn't seen as a routine), and I avoid implying natural ability. As a manager, you have little direct control over someone's talents; all you can do is motivate how those talents are applied. Telling someone they did a really good job because they are smart will imply that they didn't have to put in much effort, whereas it is increased effort that you want to encourage. Therefore, when offering praise, try to focus on their behaviour rather than their talent. For example, say 'Well done, I appreciate you working so hard to achieve that result,' instead of 'Well done, you're very good at that.'

A pat on the back by your boss for good work done provides a nice boost, but public recognition by your peers can be even more motivating. Peer-to-peer awards are a great way to encourage this. In my companies, I have set up programmes that allow any employee to nominate anyone else for a small award (such as a £50 dining voucher), at any time, for any reason, without any approval. Each nomination requires a citation so that everyone knows what the individual is being recognized for, and I define categories of award to provide some structure: *Exceptional work, Amazing result, Providing great support, Terrific idea, Unsung hero, Just being awesome.* What's most important is that the peer award is made public: every nomination is shared with the whole company so that both the award and its citation are visible to everyone. I've seen how receiving one of these awards makes someone's day, but having dozens of your co-workers then leave comments like 'So well deserved' is the extra sprinkling of magic dust that makes these programmes so effective. Even if you don't have the authority to roll out something like this across your organization, you may be able to set up a smaller informal scheme within your own team or department.

What does it look like when Play, Potential and Purpose are all activated? It's when musicians talk about being 'in the groove' or athletes get into 'the zone'. This is what psychologist Mihály Csìkszentmihàlyi called 'flow':[7] those activities we do when time simply melts away. He found that individuals who frequently experienced flow were more productive and derived greater satisfaction from their work than those who didn't. Indeed, they seemed able to tap into a limitless pool of energy, and they expressed a willingness to repeat those activities in which they achieved flow even if they were not being paid to do so. These three intrinsic motivational forces form the most essential foundations for your job as a manager. Nothing else you do will have as much impact as activating your employees' own self-motivation to perform at their highest possible level. Understanding how to wield these forces effectively will help you transition from being an amateur manager who relies upon extrinsic motivators and formal authority into a highly impactful manager who finds ways for your team to gain a deep feeling of personal satisfaction from their work.

How to spot flagging motivation

Just as harnessing individuals' intrinsic motivations can boost future performance, motivations that may have powered someone's performance in the past may wane. The motivational fuel that powered the stellar high performer on your team last year won't continue to burn for ever. We all lose interest over time and, if you don't spot this in your team, results can decline and individuals end up resigning. In the worst scenario, a single demotivated individual can poison the positivity in a team and bring everyone else down. Here are five signals that can help you to spot declining motivation before it's too late:

A change in output
An unexplained decline in productivity, volume or quality may indicate an individual just isn't putting in as much effort as usual.

Warning phrases

People are unlikely to tell you explicitly they are no longer feeling motivated, so you'll have to read between the lines. Listen out for throwaway comments that might indicate a lack of interest in the job, such as 'Just tell me what you want me to do,' 'If you say so,' or 'I don't mind.' Open questions like 'How are you feeling this week?' are a great way to bring motivation issues to the surface.

An absence of questions

Engaged employees ask questions and seek advice. Someone who doesn't ask, doesn't care. When people go quiet, they are often disengaging.

A change in behaviour

For example, when someone who is normally very punctual repeatedly arrives late, when a talkative individual becomes withdrawn, when a usually healthy employee repeatedly takes sick leave without explaining why, or when you have to start chasing up someone who's previously been very responsive.

Signs of burnout

Researchers at Stanford University found that burnout causes nearly 120,000 deaths each year in the United States alone, with a $1 trillion cost to the global economy from lost productivity. Burned-out employees are 2.6 times more likely to be actively seeking a new job, and 63 per cent more likely to take a sick day.[8] Burnout is most often blamed on excessive workload, so the most common reaction is to place people on leave for a few weeks to recharge. But burnout is much deeper than simply being too busy. After all, most of us are happy to put in extra hours if we're doing something we enjoy. Toxic management practices are a more likely cause, in particular a feeling of being treated unfairly at work, a lack of role clarity, and poor communication and support from the person's manager. The warning signs to watch out for include erosive behaviours such as unhealthy eating or drinking, excessive fatigue or weariness, becoming easily annoyed or upset and expressions of 'hopelessness'. If you spot someone who seems unable to cope, who looks like they might burst into tears or have a meltdown in the office at any moment, even with a routine workload, react quickly – but don't assume it's the individual's responsibility to fix it. The first place to look for a solution is the way you're managing them. Ask yourself, what is it I'm doing that's making my staff physically and mentally unwell?

What can you do if an employee remains unmotivated?

Individuals who have lost interest and motivation in what the team is trying to achieve retreat into themselves and pull away from collaborative work. This apathy can then spread like a disease across the team once there's a perception some individuals aren't working as hard as others, so it is essential you address an unmotivated or disengaged employee quickly.

Earlier we explored how the three negative motivational forces rely on the exertion of extrinsic pressure to drive behavioural compliance: emotional pressure, economic pressure and inertia. If you've tried to motivate an employee using intrinsic forces and you feel they still aren't operating to their full potential, you may be tempted to turn to extrinsic pressures instead, such as threatening them with a punishment or offering an extra bonus to work harder. I would urge strong caution here since such actions can have unintended consequences.

Emotional pressure is the weapon of formal authority: do as I say otherwise there will be a price to pay. This may get the task done but there's little evidence it will motivate your employees to do their job to a high standard. Emotional pressure is all about avoiding the consequences, rather than gaining the benefits.

Economic pressure can act as a very real and powerful brake on performance if someone feels they are paid unfairly relative to others in the team, the company, their peers or the market. Trying to activate their intrinsic motivation will be difficult while the issue of compensation remains at the forefront of their mind, so you can't just ignore it. People only think about money when it has become a major distraction, just as a lack of coffee in the kitchen becomes the most important issue of the day for some people. The best approach for handling compensation issues is to find a way to minimize money's impact as a negative motivational force. If an employee asks for a pay increase, it's usually because they feel they are being recompensed unfairly. As their manager, you should probe deeper to find out why they feel this way. If their request stems from envy of their friends or peers, you can remind them that their salary is tied to the value of the role they perform in your organization, which might be different from that of their friends. If they feel they are underpaid relative to others doing the same job, then loop in your HR team for guidance. As we mentioned earlier, you can address dissatisfaction simply by removing its source. Offering a pay rise in itself won't directly motivate increased effort from the individual, but it will remove a powerful negative motivational force that'll smother other attempts to improve their contribution if you don't deal with it.

While it is clear that people can become highly demotivated if they feel they are underpaid relative to others, it is not the case that paying extra above what would be regarded as fair will necessarily boost motivation, effort and performance. Many managers and organizations continue to believe that bonuses can stimulate higher performance, but I doubt this is really true for the simple reason that financial rewards are entirely extrinsic. The simple act of offering a reward or bonus may even signal to workers that the task is undesirable or unenjoyable, since an additional incentive is needed to get them to do it well. When we're motivated by money, we work to get the payment, not because we enjoy the activity. This could result in less scrupulous individuals taking the quickest and easiest route to ensure they get the reward, which may then have unintended consequences for the organization. The mis-selling of payment protection insurance (PPI) was the UK's biggest ever financial scandal, with British banks paying out nearly £40 billion in compensation to customers who were wrongly sold insurance they didn't need by employees who were chasing their substantial sales bonuses.

Bonuses may deliver a short-term boost to employees' effort – just as a double espresso can charge your attention level for a couple of hours – but the effect quickly wears off. Once the reward is received, the motivational force ends, so organizations find they must institutionalize the prize, at which point it inevitably becomes expected as part of the salary package. Human psychology then makes this situation even worse, because people hate losing something they think they're entitled to more than they love gaining something they don't already have. Once an employee comes to regard receiving a bonus as the norm, taking that bonus away becomes even more demotivating than if it had never been offered in the first place.

If you do want to offer a bonus, then there's a way to use the principle of loss aversion to your advantage. A team of researchers including renowned behavioural economist Steven Levitt found that teachers who are given a bonus at the beginning of the school year that must be returned if they fail to meet their target by the end of the year improve the performance of their students significantly more than teachers who are offered an end-of-year bonus contingent on meeting the same goals.[9]

If someone is simply lethargic through inertia – unwilling to move away from the status quo – then your only option will be to give them a push to create momentum. I've seen this situation many times with individuals who remain in jobs they don't enjoy, working for managers they loathe, simply because they are afraid of change. People generally like stability and predictability; they fear change because it presents a different and unknown future to the one that they are expecting. Even if that future is likely to be brighter and happier than the present, people still seem to prefer the stability of the known over the uncertainty of the unknown. One way to unfreeze people in these situations is to remove any mental barriers they might have. A simple conversation to allay their fears and paint a picture of what their new future will look like might be all that's needed. If you find an employee is simply bored with their job, then you could re-energize them by moving them into a new role, giving them a new project that aligns with their interests, or changing the clients they manage.

Give your team a motivation audit

To understand how motivated your team feels, especially if you're inheriting a new team you haven't worked with before, it might be worth undertaking an employee survey to understand how they each feel towards their job and the organization as a whole. Armed with this information, you'll be able to prioritize what's most important and urgent to address.

For a sample questionnaire you can use, please visit www.managingpeople.tips.

....

Chapter takeaways

- Why we work determines how well we work. You'll need to provide the inspiration that motivates your employees to want to do the best job possible.

- Beware of relying on the power that's derived from the formal authority associated with your position in the hierarchy of the organization.

- Informal authority is a much more effective form of influence as it stems from your interpersonal relationships with others.

- Intrinsic motivation is the most powerful tool in your armoury as a manager and comprises three forces: Play, Potential and Purpose:

Motivational force	Delivery method	Employee benefits
Play	Interesting work	Assigned tasks they'll enjoy
	Autonomy	Empowered to operate in the way they prefer
	Flexible working	Maximized productivity
Potential	Mastery	Doing activities they're naturally good at
	Ambition	Opportunity to upskill
Purpose	Impact storytelling	Delivering value to others
	Passion	Enhanced motivation to perform well

- Avoid extrinsic motivations that force people to do things they ordinarily wouldn't choose to do: emotional pressure, economic pressure and inertia.

Step 2: Define and Track Expectations

Manage with the end in mind

In this chapter we'll focus on the setting of goals for each employee and pick up some tips for running best-practice performance-management discussions you can use to track progress. Your team members need to know what you want them to do and how well they are doing. Without this clarity, they can't prioritize their work or see how much progress and how big an impact they are making. You'll also need to have some way of assessing whether they are doing the job as you expect, otherwise you will be unable to offer tailored personal development support. The collective impact of failing to define and track expectations will be a decline in your team's intrinsic motivation.

Setting expectations

When thinking about what you want each of your employees to achieve, there are two aspects to everyone's job you should consider:

Objectives

These are the reasons each job in your team exists. Objectives are tied to the *role*: for example, to increase website traffic, generate sales, deliver good service to customers, conduct research, manage projects.

....

Results

These are the outputs you expect each employee to achieve against each objective. These can also be referred to as targets or key performance indicators (KPIs). KPIs are tied to the *individual* doing the job: what each person is expected to achieve within their respective roles.

Some organizations refer to these in combination as OKRs: objectives and key results. Taken together, these form an individual's *expectations*: what work you want them to do and what you expect them to deliver.

Setting clear expectations for your team drives stronger performance because it defines what the organization needs each person to achieve and why, stretches each person by giving them something to aim for, enables prioritization of time and effort and provides you with a methodology for measuring their progress. Without these, most employees will default to working within their comfort zone, doing work they most enjoy, relying on their perception of what's most important rather than what's actually best for the organization.

When setting the objectives for a role, you should begin by defining the core strategic priorities for each job. These are the primary areas of value the role is expected to contribute to the business. These 'big rocks' are often significant in scope and take a great deal of effort to move forward, but they deliver substantial impact when they land. Remember that objectives should be based on the organization's requirements from each role and not scoped around the capabilities of the person doing it.

Ideally, a role's objectives will already have been outlined for you in its job description. But poorly written job descriptions are often filled with a list of tasks rather than objectives, so you may need to step back and define these yourself. A great way to figure out what the big rocks should be for each role in your team is by completing this sentence:

'*The reason the company created this job is to . . .*'

Your job as a manager is to define the what, not the how. Objectives should specify only what the business requires each to achieve. This will empower the individual by giving them autonomy – a key driver of positive intrinsic motivation. (Explaining to an employee *how* to do their job falls under the remit of training and coaching, which we'll cover in the next chapter.)

It's a good idea to emphasize *why* each of the objectives matters as this will help the individual understand how their work contributes to wider goals, which in turn should engage their Purpose motivation lever. Because senior executives spend all day thinking about strategy and the reasons certain decisions are made, it is easy to forget that others aren't exposed to these discussions. The *why* often gets left out of the objective-setting process and managers can fail to effectively explain how each person's work has impact beyond their bubble.

Try to give each employee only three or four objectives, each of which should be easily understood, and offer quick feedback loops so you can track progress easily. Restricting yourself like this will keep both of you fully focused on the most important core areas of responsibility. For example, the core objectives for an e-commerce manager might be:

1 Grow the volume of visitors to the website.

2 Increase the percentage of site visitors who make a purchase.

3 Increase the average order value for each customer.

Notice that these objectives do not specify how these should be achieved – that's for the individual in the role to decide.

To avoid any ambiguity over what results you are expecting, each objective should be accompanied by a target – a KPI. These KPIs are the anticipated outcomes from each objective and should complete this sentence:

'*I expect you to deliver . . .*'

When thinking about defining KPIs, consider these five ways to assess output:

- **Quantity:** The volume of work required, such as units sold, calls answered or revenue generated.

- **Quality:** A measure of how good the employee's work is, such as positive customer feedback, number of returned items, accuracy of spelling and grammar, or conversion rate of quotes to orders.

- **Cost:** What's the maximum budget they have to spend, or target cost per unit sold?

- **Deadline:** When do the results have to be achieved by?

- **Behaviours:** How do you expect them to achieve the KPIs you have set (e.g. 'while adhering to guidelines' or 'by working collaboratively with others')?

Ideally, each KPI you set should be specific and timebound and should include a *from* metric as well as a *to* metric so that they provide a record of how much progress has been made. For example:

1 Grow the volume of visitors to the website from 125,000 per week to 140,000 per week by 31 December.

2 Increase the percentage of site visitors who make a purchase from 2.5% to 2.9% by 31 December.

3 Increase the average order value for each customer from £31.35 to £35.00 by 31 December.

Of course, not all roles or objectives can be easily assigned quantitative metrics. In these cases, still try to use the framework of quantity, quality, cost, deadline and behaviours to describe in words what you think excellent performance would look like for each employee.

By setting KPIs based on what the organization needs from the individual in order to achieve its corporate targets (known as top-down goal setting), rather than what the employee thinks they can achieve (known as bottom-up goal setting), you'll avoid the risk of your team failing to deliver its collective objectives. Making a KPI 'uncomfortable', by introducing a stretch beyond what the employee might voluntarily propose, is a really good approach. Ambitious goals pull people out of their comfort zone, which should then deliver both greater motivation and better results. However, be cautious that any stretch you create does not make the goal appear unattainable as this could have the opposite effect, destroying motivation and creating stress. It might also promote unethical or unwanted behaviours as people are forced to find creative ways to avoid failing. A good balance is to define a set of achievable KPIs as your base (minimum) expectation, plus a set of stretch KPIs that you'll recognize as outstanding performance. I've found a two-monthly schedule to achieve these KPIs is about right. The world is simply too dynamic and fast-moving to be able to set in stone priorities for extended periods.

If you find it hard to determine what KPIs to set for a particular objective, try completing these sentences to help bring the individual's job into clearer focus:

- To deliver the overall business/team objectives, this person needs to achieve . . .

- To be regarded as successful in this job, this person needs to . . .

- I'll regard it as a great result if this person is able to . . .

Once you have a draft set of objectives and KPIs, it's time to discuss them with each employee to solicit their input. It's important they accept the expectations you set them, otherwise they won't be motivated. If there's a wide gap between your proposed KPIs and what the employee thinks they can achieve then this may highlight either a gap in their perceived capabilities, a gap in resources (such as budget), or unrealistic corporate expectations – all of which are worth you knowing and addressing at the start, rather than after your targets have been missed.

Reviewing progress during one-to-one meetings

Regular check-in meetings with each of your direct reports should be an essential part of your schedule. These are the best, and easiest, way to regularly review performance against the expectations you've set. They'll also provide a motivation boost to the employee. After all, there's little value in reaching the end of a performance period only to discover your employees didn't achieve what you were expecting. Make time for these; cancelling or postponing a meeting without good reason signals to someone that you consider them a low priority. I regard half an hour every two weeks is the minimum amount of time to offer effective support. More junior or newly hired team members may need longer.

Here's how you can make your one-to-one meetings really valuable for both you and your employees:

Review progress against goals

Don't let underperformance be a surprise, or let over-performance go unremarked upon. Check-in meetings every fortnight will help ensure the employee keeps their goals in focus and allow you to make a course correction if things aren't going to plan.

Receive a general work update

The employee can update you on their progress and achievements beyond their core goals, which I find frequently then broadens out into opportunities for advice or guidance. This can identify wider issues that might be holding them back, or new opportunities that would benefit from your support.

Provide feedback

Highlight aspects of their work that you want them to pay closer attention to but which don't warrant a separate discussion. How to give great feedback is covered in more detail in the next chapter.

Boost their self-esteem

Keep employees motivated by delivering praise, recognition and gratitude, and reinforcing your belief in them and your desire to help them succeed in their career.

Reinforce why their job matters

Stimulate their intrinsic motivation by reminding them of the value of their work and contribution to the broader goals of the organization.

Check-in on morale

If you regularly ask your employees whether they are enjoying their job, it shows you care about their motivation and you stand a better chance of identifying potential discontent before it festers or escalates.

Invest in your relationship

If nothing else, one-to-one time with your employees will help you to understand each other better and build a more effective working relationship. Your employees will want to spend more time with you than you might expect.

A trick for ensuring every one-to-one meeting is a good use of time is to regard it as the employee's meeting and not yours. Seeing it as an opportunity for them to solicit your guidance will prevent these meetings becoming solely a channel for one-way communication in which you receive updates or lay down instructions. Open questions are a great way to expand dialogue beyond day-to-day work activities:

- 'How are things going?'

- 'What's on your mind at the moment?'

- 'How are you feeling?'

- 'What's holding you back?'

- 'What's frustrating you?'

- 'What do you find most interesting?'

- 'How could we use your talents better?'

- 'How can I be most useful to you right now?'

- 'What feedback do you have for me?'

- 'How can I support you better?'

Performance appraisals

Performance reviews or appraisals are a tool to formally assess how well an individual has delivered against the goals that you set for them. They can be standalone for the benefit of an individual employee or run as part of a company-wide process on a quarterly, half-yearly or annual schedule. They are intended to answer the questions 'How well is each employee doing against expectations?' and 'How is each employee performing relative to others in the organization?'

Unfortunately, many corporate appraisal processes fail to deliver more than a set of performance metrics for senior management. In a recent survey of business executives by Deloitte, more than half the responders questioned (58 per cent) believed that their current performance-management approach drives neither stronger employee engagement nor higher performance.[1] That's a real shame because appraisals that are executed well can and should be valuable for the employee and help to stimulate greater motivation. You can avoid becoming a manager whose appraisals are viewed as a waste of time by following some simple best practices.

The most useful appraisals happen when both the manager and employee have prepared for them and understand their value. As a manager, if you don't do your homework in advance, you'll risk delivering unsubstantiated opinions, confused or conflicting feedback or insensitive or unhelpful criticism. You may even end up failing to deliver key messages that the employee needs to hear, whether those are good or bad. Equally, if the employee hasn't had a chance to prepare their own self-review, then they won't have consciously thought about their own performance achievements and you won't be able to identify any gaps between how the employee thinks they have performed and what your own opinion is.

Here are a few approaches that will help your appraisal meetings deliver positive impact for everyone involved:

Communicate the value in advance
Let your team know that you're committed to supporting their development and that the appraisal process is a critical mechanism to help them understand how they are doing, what's working well and what isn't, and identify where you can help them to achieve their maximum potential.

Seek the opinion of others who know the employee's work better than you
Soliciting feedback in advance from some of the employee's peers and customers (internal or external) will allow

you to form a fully rounded view of their performance. Like school children in front of the headmaster, everyone's on their best behaviour in front of their manager. You may hear a different side to a person's achievements, behaviours and attitudes by talking to those who spend more time actually working with them.

....

Have a clear structure

In your review meeting or appraisal document, structure your feedback around *achievements* (how they did against their KPIs), *superpowers* (what they are really good at), and *development areas* (where they could become better). In the achievements section, discuss their performance against each objective and goal that you set so that you don't allow an overall opinion of underperformance to cloud the fact they did some things well.

....

Be clear on where their performance didn't meet your expectations

The benefit of setting KPIs is that a discussion on underperformance can be objective and not based solely on your opinion. The best feedback is always backed up by solid examples or good evidence.

....

Assess their performance, not their personality

Remember that you are not assessing the quality of the person or whether you like them. You are evaluating how well the individual performed the job they were tasked with. Your comments about behaviours, in particular, should not flow into an assessment of the individual's character. For example, rather than assert they 'have a bad attitude', focus on how they repeatedly arrive late to work.

Understand the context

Explore the reasons for any underperformance by asking open questions such as 'Why do you think things didn't go as planned?' The employee will feel more fairly judged if any external factors beyond their control have been taken into account.

Identify performance constraints

Include a discussion on how you could help unlock better performance. Questions like 'What's holding you back?' and 'What could I or others do differently to help you become more successful?' can be very effective at identifying constraints on an employee's performance that could be easily rectified.

Create a vision for their future

Try to help the employee understand what their future looks like by including a discussion around their growth trajectory and career path. For example, when might they be ready for a promotion and what could they do to keep on that path? While it might be disappointing for an ambitious individual to hear they aren't where they thought they were, it's better to be transparent about this and prompt a discussion of how they might close the gap rather than leaving the employee with unrealistic expectations that will set them up for disappointment and resentment in the future.

Agree actions

Close by agreeing what you will do as their manager to support the employee's continuous development and what they will take responsibility for actioning themselves. Be sure to follow through on your commitments – failing to do so will destroy their trust in both you and the appraisal process.

Many corporate appraisal processes fail because they are regarded as tick-box exercises that allow weak managers to assume performance discussions only need to happen during appraisals, and they use this as an excuse (consciously or not) to avoid having difficult conversations with employees outside these infrequent, formal meetings. Consequently, the content of appraisals is often a surprise to employees. Please don't fall into this trap. The best managers have frequent and regular conversations with their team members about performance. Appraisal meetings should simply summarize what's already been discussed during the period in question; nothing should come as a nasty surprise to the employee. If they have done well, you should have already showered the employee with praise and recognition to turn up their intrinsic motivation to the max during the appraisal period. If they have not met your expectations, it's too late to do anything about it if the first they know of it is the appraisal meeting at the end of the period. Providing constant feedback throughout the appraisal period is the only way you can help employees maintain alignment with their objectives and continually reinforce their intrinsic motivation.

Handling underperformance

Even with quantitative KPIs, performance appraisal meetings and their accompanying documentation will still involve sharing your opinion of the employee's contribution. There's no getting round this. So the way you deliver your feedback is critical in determining how it is received by the employee and whether it motivates any change in behaviour. Research by the Corporate Leadership Council across 19,000 managers in thirty-four companies found that an emphasis on performance weaknesses in appraisals reduces subsequent performance by 26 per cent.[2] But underperformance still needs to be addressed, so how do you do this in a way that supports motivation rather than destroys it?

In his book *How to Be Good at Performance Appraisals*, Dick Grote describes three groups of people:

- **A players:** The team's top performers.

- **B players:** The steady contributors.

- **C players:** The underperformers.

Because they are the highest achievers, A players constantly worry about underperforming. They are used to excelling at everything and the smallest failure can seem a huge knockback. Your B players, meanwhile, have the self-awareness to realize they aren't as strong as the As and so they constantly worry that you regard them as an underachiever. They work hard to ensure they meet expectations but see a fine line between meeting goals and just missing them. Meanwhile, C players lack the self-awareness to appreciate how poorly they perform relative to everyone else, so they perceive themselves as strong contributors. In other words, As are afraid they will be considered Bs. The Bs are scared you think they're Cs. And the Cs are convinced they are A players.

Giving any negative feedback to As will reinforce their conviction they are Bs. No matter how much positive news you give them, A players will leave the meeting remembering only these. They'll return to their desks deflated, thinking it was a terrible review. Similarly, telling B players they didn't meet expectations will confirm their fears that in your eyes they are underperformers, further lowering their self-esteem. Meanwhile, C players will ignore anything negative because this information won't align with the impression they have of themselves, and instead they'll take any positive feedback you give them as confirmation they are as great as they believe they are.

Therefore, when considering what to focus on in the actual face-to-face appraisal meeting, you'll need to adopt a nuanced approach that takes into account the employee's opinion of their own performance.

For those who set themselves high standards and are worried you might think they're underperforming (your A and B players), deliver only positive feedback. You want their meetings to be highly motivational so that they walk out of the room on a high. Focus only on what they are great at and how they can further leverage these strengths to deliver even more impact. Since they are an A or B player, any development needs are likely to be relatively minor, so postpone any discussions around these to a separate, less formal meeting, such as a one-to-one catch-up.

For those whose work has not been good enough, especially those who fail to recognize they are not performing as you expect (your C players), keep the whole meeting focused on the areas in which they need to improve. Those who believe they are better than they actually are will be seeking confirmation of this self-image, so avoid feeding them anything they can use to do so. Instead, set clear expectations from the start of the meeting with a statement such as: 'I need to tell you that your performance has not met my expectations, so I want to spend our time together exploring what hasn't gone well and discussing how we can work together to improve your contribution.' You'll want to be fair to the employee, so the meeting can still be very positive and motivating. Those who recognize they aren't succeeding should appreciate your offer to help them get better. Those who don't will need to hear a very clear message from you.

Hearing that your manager is disappointed with your performance will dent anyone's confidence. Constructive feedback, on the other hand, offers guidance on what or how the employee can do better next time. Understanding how to improve, and having your manager's support to achieve this, will prevent an employee's injured morale from suffering further damage. Every piece of negative feedback you give should always be accompanied by ideas on what to do differently next time. If you combine your candid feedback with a productive discussion on what they can do to address their underperformance and how you can help them improve, the employee can actually leave the meeting positive about the future. Of course, if you're following the advice in this book, genuine underperformance should already have been addressed before the appraisal meeting in your regular one-to-ones. Remember: no nasty surprises.

If the sub-performance resulted from a deficiency in skills, competency or experience, then the only way the individual can improve is through personal development. Development is the third pillar of my managerial framework, and in the next chapter we'll explore best practices for providing feedback and helping employees to improve their performance.

··

Chapter takeaways

- When setting expectations for your employees, split these into *objectives* and *results*. Together, these define what success looks like for each person.

- If you also set specific, stretch goals, your employees are much more likely to deliver higher performance than if you just urge them to do their best.

- Defining *what* you want done without saying *how* you want it done will empower your team through autonomy.

- Reviewing progress on a regular basis in one-to-one meetings allows you to course correct and ensure there are no unpleasant surprises during more formal review meetings.

- To ensure appraisals are valuable, you should commit time in advance to prepare for them, seek input from others, use objective data and examples to avoid basing feedback on opinion, and discuss what both of you can do to help the individual be even more successful in the next period.

- For employees who set high expectations for themselves, reinforce and encourage them by focusing on their successes. For employees who don't realize, or don't care, that they are underperforming, be clear on what didn't go to plan and identify what they, or you, should do differently next time.

Step 3: Develop Your Employees

How to improve performance

Personal development is, quite simply, one of the highest-leverage activities a manager can invest time in. A small amount of your day given over to developing your employees' skills or experience can create substantial improvements in their long-term contributions. There are few other things you can do as a manager that will deliver a greater return on investment.

In Step 2 we covered how to define, communicate and track the output you expect from each employee. This is a critical first stage in improving performance because it ensures each employee knows what they must achieve. If you've also incorporated some stretch, it will encourage them to push themselves beyond their comfort zone.

In this chapter, we'll cover what you can do if there's a gap between what the employee has achieved or feels able to deliver and what you require from them. Letting an employee know in an appraisal that they have failed to meet your expectations will not, in itself, improve their subsequent performance. It's no use just telling them they did a bad job. Identifying *why* a person underdelivered and then helping them to address the gap in skills, knowledge, experience, motivation or behaviour that caused their underperformance will be the only way you can actually improve their future contributions. As their manager, it'll be up to you to guide their personal development proactively – they'll be unlikely to improve otherwise.

There are five tools you can use as a manager to improve the quality of someone's performance. Together, they will help you to develop your employees' capabilities:

1 **Feedback:** Feedback helps employees to understand what they have done well and what hasn't worked out as expected. It boosts their self-awareness and allows them to focus their efforts in the right areas. Feedback is backward facing, since it addresses what an employee did in the past.

2 **Training:** If an individual doesn't have the skill, knowledge or experience required to take their performance to the next level, then you'll need to help them acquire it. Training sets people up for success by giving them the expertise that they do not currently have but which they need in order to do their job effectively. Since training is the transfer of knowledge from one person to another, it is usually created and delivered by a subject-matter expert.

3 **Coaching:** This can be used to improve future performance by helping the employee to apply their existing knowledge in new ways. Coaching helps an employee think through problems and can be delivered impromptu during one-to-one meetings, or within dedicated coaching sessions. It's most effective if the individual already has the necessary skills or experience and just needs extra help to structure their thoughts.

4 **Mentoring:** Individuals who just want help to polish their performance can benefit from being inspired and guided by someone who has already achieved success in a similar role. Mentoring involves the sharing of your personal experience and industry knowledge with someone who is less experienced.

5 **Counselling:** This is used to address a specific root cause of performance issues, often related to interpersonal communication, relationships or emotions.

The first four tools – feedback, training, coaching and mentoring – are all skills you'll need to master to become a superstar manager who is able to extract the best performance from your team. I won't cover counselling in this book as this is a highly specialist activity that's best left to properly trained and qualified individuals.

How to give effective feedback

Providing feedback to your employees is a core responsibility of a manager. Without feedback on what they've done well, your employees will feel you aren't recognizing their contributions and their morale will decline. Without feedback on work they have done poorly, individuals won't know they're failing to meet your expectations or how they need to improve.

Well-rounded feedback is surprisingly hard to give. I've experienced managers who give praise freely but struggle to deliver the right messages when something's not working properly. These managers are often loved by their employees but aren't great at dealing with problems. There are also managers who are very open with their criticism but rarely praise good work. These managers can achieve great results because of the high standards they set, but this comes at the cost of terrible team morale. Then there are the managers who offer no feedback at all, who find giving any opinion exceptionally awkward, even if that feedback is positive. These are the managers who wait until the episodic appraisal meeting to let an employee know how they've done.

To be successful, it's essential that you become comfortable offering every type of feedback to your team. It is such a critical foundation for motivation and performance improvement that it's something you must force yourself to do, even if it doesn't come naturally. It really does become much easier the more often you do it, especially as you come to realize how much employees want and value your opinion and advice. When you deliver feedback in an effective way, you should find that the positive reactions from your team stimulate your own intrinsic motivation because of the difference you'll be making to their working lives.

Giving feedback shouldn't always be a negative experience for the person receiving it. If you only ever use it as a way to deliver bad news, your employees will become anxious every time you ask to have a word with them. So, for each piece of negative feedback you give, try to offer five pieces of praise. While that might be hard to achieve for staff who are underperforming, it's a useful way for you to seek out opportunities to recognize good-quality work or effort, especially if you're the kind of person who feels awkward offering praise. Even if someone's output is below what you required, you can still offer praise if they were at least trying their best. A person who is appreciated will always do more than expected. Being praised in front of others, especially your peers, can deliver a huge boost to an individual's self-esteem and confidence, while also motivating the rest of the team to strive for similar recognition. Such recognition is especially important for A and B players, since providing regular praise acts as a reminder that you still regard them as high achievers and will help counter the self-doubt generated by the lofty standards they set for themselves. The impact will be even greater if this recognition is unexpected and comes as a nice surprise.

To deliver five pieces of praise for every item of criticism, look out for opportunities to offer a compliment. Recognize when someone is doing something difficult that requires them to make an extra effort, take a risk, or push themselves beyond their comfort zone. If they are trying something different, show them you've noticed. Regardless of how it turns out, let them know you respect them for having a go. No matter how senior or junior someone is, people want to know that their manager cares about their work. An expression of thanks for delivering good work, no matter how small, creates enormous motivational benefits – and it costs nothing.

Get into the habit of giving timely feedback, rather than storing it up until your next one-to-one meeting. In any educational environment, be it taking driving lessons, mastering a new language or becoming a chef, learning is deepest when you receive immediate, clear feedback after each attempt. Imagine sitting next to a driving instructor who gave you no feedback until the end of your course of lessons. Not only would you probably have crashed the car, you would have had no opportunity to apply their advice during the lessons. Learning a sport or practical skill, whether it's windsurfing, carpentry or playing the piano, relies upon immediate feedback from your teacher or coach for you to know what you're doing wrong and how to put it right.

If you've ever owned a pet, you'll know that rewards must be given straight after the good behaviour in order for the mental associations to be made. In a work environment, it is similarly important to deliver feedback as soon as possible after the incident that prompted it. Pulling a team member aside immediately after an event in which their performance didn't meet your standards is far better than waiting until your next one-to-one meeting, by which time either you or the individual might have forgotten about the incident entirely.

Once you have decided that feedback needs to be given, choose an appropriate time and place. Don't delay, but don't rush either. If tempers are high and you're both feeling emotional, it's probably best to allow a cooling-off period. You don't want what you say to be driven by your own emotional reaction to the situation, nor do you want the recipient to be in an elevated emotional state when they receive your feedback. Instead, consider addressing the problem at the end of the day before the person leaves to go home, or, if that's not practical, first thing the following day. Always respect the employee's privacy and avoid delivering negative feedback in front of others. Top tip: *praise in public, criticize in private.*

Giving developmental feedback

Badly delivered comments about underperformance can harm or destroy relationships, especially those that might have been fragile to begin with. While praise is often associated with results, criticism is frequently related to behaviour, which is highly personal. It's why both deliverer and recipient can feel anxious, each fearful they might get emotional, say the wrong thing or trigger a reaction that will make things worse. To minimize this, I always try to regard this type of feedback as *developmental*: intended to help the individual improve rather than just to deliver criticism. Developmental feedback is the only way people learn what is diminishing their performance so that they might have a chance to address it. Not being honest and direct about poor performance simply cheats the employee out of a chance to improve.

Adopting this mindset will help you to ensure your comments are focused as much on how the person could become better as on what they did wrong. When delivered well, developmental feedback can strengthen trust, respect, collaboration and motivation. By including clear suggestions on how things could be improved or handled differently, you can create a positive interaction because everyone appreciates being given the opportunity to address their flaws. Your team will learn to value your directness and their self-awareness will benefit from your observations. I once had an employee who would ramble during conference calls, preventing others from speaking. It was her blind spot: she didn't know she was doing it, or that it was a problem. When I told her, she realized that she was interpreting the momentary silence after she finished speaking as a sign that the person on the end of the line had not understood her, so she kept repeating herself. This was partly a cultural issue: in her own society, she was used to talking until she was interrupted. She hadn't appreciated that in a more reserved culture people might think it rude to interrupt. She was very grateful for my feedback, which she still recalls ten years later as something that continues to guide her.

If you're uncomfortable delivering developmental feedback because you're unsure what to say, try following this simple framework to craft your message so that it is objective and easily understood by the recipient:

1 **Find the right time and place:** Feedback should be timely, but also private. I find it's often easier to have awkward conversations while walking rather than facing

someone across a meeting-room table. Because you aren't forced to look the other person in the eye, it is less confrontational and it's harder for emotions to cloud and distract the discussion.

2 **Begin by asking permission:** Explain you wish to share some feedback and check that's OK with them. They may have a good reason for saying no – rushing to an appointment, for example – and this simple question sets a serious mood for the conversation so that they know it isn't a normal chat.

3 **Frame the situation:** Frame the message by providing the context for why you need to give them this feedback. For example, 'I'd like to discuss how you handled yesterday's meeting with the client.'

4 **Describe their behaviour:** Explain what you observed that did not meet the standards you expected. Be specific and avoid generalizations like 'You always . . .' or 'You never . . .' which are just opinionated complaints and not problem statements. Simply state the facts of what happened. For example, 'You may not have realized this, but you repeatedly interrupted the client when they were explaining why they are cancelling their contract.'

5 **Explain the impact:** Explain why you felt this behaviour was unacceptable. What was the effect on you or someone else? Here you can use emotive words, if appropriate, to help the individual visualize and appreciate the consequences of what they did. For example, 'I felt this was disrespectful and I could see that the client was getting very irritated.'

6 **Seek acceptance:** Check that the employee has fully understood your feedback and ask if they feel that your comments are fair. You're not asking if they agree with you. Don't feel you have to justify your opinion. You can acknowledge that their intention was probably different from the actual impact, but by stating facts, especially as they affect others, it'll be harder for the employee to push back. If they accept your feedback, even if they disagree with it, they are more likely to act on your comments after the meeting.

7 **Provide a solution:** Help the individual visualize how they could have handled the situation differently and prompt them to consider how they should change their approach in the future. You could do this by asking them directly: 'How do you think you could have handled that better?' Or you could be more prescriptive: 'I'd like you to focus on improving your active listening skills so that you really appreciate what other people are saying before you offer your opinion. How do you think you could get into that habit?'

8 **Agreement:** At the end of the discussion, I always like to reiterate what we have discussed to ensure the message has fully landed and the employee has internalized why their behaviour or performance was unacceptable and what I want them to do differently next time. Asking for their agreement and commitment to the proposed solution will increase the chances they will follow through. If the issue is sufficiently serious, summarize in writing what's been said so you have it documented for future reference if needed.

9 **End with encouragement:** If you state your confidence that the person you're giving feedback to will be able to improve, they'll be more likely to leave the meeting with a positive feeling, not filled with resentment, negativity and humiliation. It will also help you maintain a level of trust and respect from your team if they know you have their backs and are truly committed to their success. I always finish with a comment like 'I want to help you to do your best.' If they mention a challenge or issue that they'd like you to resolve, be sure to follow through and report back to them when it has been done.

An easy way to remember this framework when you're in a feedback situation is the acronym COIN:

- Context – what's prompted the need to give feedback.

- Observation – what the employee did.

- Impact – what the impact was.

- Next steps – what you want the employee to do as a consequence.

When offering developmental feedback, always treat the recipient with dignity and respect. Discuss only performance issues, not their personality or character. Mention only observed facts or behaviours, not assumptions, and support your assertions with evidence. If the issue in focus is the employee's attitude or behaviour, try to find a way to tie it directly and specifically to a performance issue, such as the impact their attitude has on others. By asking why they behave as they do, you might uncover an underlying cause. Personal issues at home, a personality clash with someone in the team, financial or health problems – these can all unintentionally shape our attitude at work. Sometimes, when a negative attitude is questioned, an employee will acknowledge the real issue, explain how it might have come about and accept they need to resolve it.

Finally, a word of caution about documenting what has been said in a performance-improvement situation. Most disciplinary disputes will inevitably require the submission of all written correspondence regarding an employee's underperformance. What you say in an email to the employee, your HR department or others could be used as evidence to support an unfair dismissal or bullying claim. Reviewing all your emails and documents through the lens of 'Would I be happy for this to be shown to the employee or read out in court?' before you press send may help you to avoid messy situations in the future.

Handling emotional reactions

You'll regularly have to deal with all types of emotional situations as a manager, either because someone has reacted to something you or others have done, or you've reacted emotionally to the actions of others. The most common reactions that will require your attention will be anger, distress and defensiveness. Despite it rarely being anyone's intention to upset others, especially in a professional context, these reactions do have a major effect on people's relationships and their motivation to perform well. This is especially true if an employee has reacted badly to something their manager has done. Whether or not you had good or bad intentions, the result is the same – their trust in you will be damaged and the individual will feel less secure and comfortable around you.

'Emotional intelligence' is the term used to describe how well a person perceives and handles emotions, both in themselves and in others. Mastering this skill will help you to manage conflict resolution and become more in-tune with the inevitable ups and downs of your team. It encompasses four key areas:

- **Self-awareness:** Having an awareness of what your own emotional triggers are.

- **Self-management:** The ability to keep your own emotions in check when they become disrupted.

- **Empathy:** Being able to read the emotions of others and respond appropriately.

- **Social skills:** Interacting and communicating with others in ways that are sensitive to their feelings.

While emotional intelligence is not something everyone will possess at the start of a managerial role, it is a skill you can work on and improve by knowing what to look out for and developing an appreciation of how to handle different reactions. Strong emotional intelligence sets great managers apart from merely good managers. Becoming hyper-conscious of how everything you say and do may be interpreted will make you both a better communicator and a more sensitive manager who is able to develop higher levels of trust with your employees.

Emails are a minefield for potential miscommunication because you can offer no supporting signals such as tone or body language to help the receiver understand the context of a message. It's so easy to become upset or angry at an email when this really was not the intention of the sender. If someone has reacted badly to an email they've received, I'll ask them to review again what was actually written. Do the words support the reader's interpretation unequivocally, or could the message be read in an entirely different way if they are untangled from the reader's cognitive biases and subconscious assumptions? Is what they assumed the sender meant supported by what was actually written? Asking them to separate the objective elements from their subjective interpretation of them is a great way to defuse these types of emotional situations. This approach can also be used to address unintended emotional reactions to both verbal communication and behaviour. If I find myself responding emotionally to a situation, I will try to create a timeout – for example, by walking away or closing the email and not reading it again until the following day – so that I can respond in a more objective way once my initial emotions have subsided.

When giving developmental feedback, you should expect the other party to react emotionally. It's hard not to when you're told you're not as a good as you thought you were. Here are a few ways you can avoid triggering a strong emotional reaction during an appraisal and strategies to deal with one if you do:

Make your written messages transparent

Because most emotional reactions stem from misinterpretation, try to spot ways in which your messages might be ambiguous. Emoji icons have become so popular in messaging apps and email precisely because they allow the sender to provide clues as to how they want the reader to interpret their written words – a winky icon to indicate you may not mean exactly what you've said or a smiley icon to let the reader know you're not angry. Emojis may not be appropriate in your workplace, so instead ensure that your message makes it absolutely clear what you mean and isn't open to a different interpretation. Being candid may feel overly direct, but at least your audience should understand exactly what you mean.

Empathize with how the recipient might be feeling

If you're communicating with someone who is already in a heightened emotional state, whatever you say will be viewed through this lens. If someone's angry, your words may simply fuel their anger. If they're upset, ignoring their distress will make you look unsympathetic and worsen the situation. Explicitly acknowledging how you think the other party is feeling will demonstrate empathy, which should encourage them to relax and consider what you say from another angle. Asking what's caused them to become upset or angry will open up a dialogue about whether what was said or done warranted such a reaction.

Remain objective when responding

Supporting your assertions with undeniable facts will encourage the other party to listen to these statements and not overlay them with their own assumptions and interpretations. They might think you're constantly picking on them when actually you're just highlighting a few important development areas with good intentions, and are doing this for every employee.

Encourage the other party to be objective

Even if someone isn't showing an emotional reaction, they might still be fuming or crying inside. You can address this by asking them if they feel your comments are fair or asking how they feel about what you've just said.

Find common ground

Whatever the situation, it's likely that both of you will have a common interest in creating a win–win outcome.

The other party will want to become less upset/angry, and you'll want them to address whatever performance issues you may have highlighted. Tell them you want to resolve this situation to the benefit of both of you. You can salvage trust if they feel you are genuinely interested in understanding their point of view. Remind them that you have their best interests at heart, and that you think they have the potential to be great if they work on these areas of personal development.

Supporting development through training

Training is to managers what compound interest is to investors. It is the gift that keeps giving, and the return on investment increases over time. It involves the transfer of knowledge from one person to another and can be implemented in four ways:

Deliver the training internally
Someone in your organization, including you, may have the skills or experience that would address the employee's knowledge gap. Work-shadowing assignments or 'lunch and learn' workshops are a great way to share expertise.

Third party in-person training courses
This is what most people default to when training needs are discussed. However, training courses can be very expensive and I have often found them less effective than other approaches because what's taught doesn't take account of each participant's individual needs and context. Knowledge retention is most effective when practice immediately follows

learning, but the timing of training courses means many participants don't have an opportunity to action what they have learnt before it is forgotten.

....

Distance learning online

Online training can be deployed 'just-in-time' so that it is undertaken at the stage when it is most relevant to a person's job. However, it is only effective if the individual is actively engaged in the learning process, which is why I regard it as a self-learning approach. When engagement is passive, such as those online courses related to corporate policies or legal compliance, learning is very limited. The most long-term value comes when the employee is self-motivated to learn.

....

Self-teaching

The desire to become an expert in something is one of the core elements of intrinsic motivation and is the best way to learn, since the student's mind is already curious and interested in the subject. Individuals in this heightened motivational state will naturally seek out ways to deepen their knowledge, usually without needing help from their manager. That's why I regard self-teaching as the most effective training option – it's the reason that educational videos on YouTube are so popular.

Teachers can teach only if the student is willing to study. Training will deliver long-term value only if the individual being trained is self-motivated to learn. A great way to test this is to ask if they would be willing to contribute towards the cost or undertake the training in their own time. Individuals who invest their time or money alongside the organization will have far more motivation to get value from it. If an employee asks to go on a training course, I'll ask what other avenues they've already explored to learn on their own. For example, if someone asks to go on a sales course, I'll ask them what books they have already read on the topic. If an individual wants to develop their presentation skills, I'll ask them what YouTube videos they have watched on the subject. If they haven't made the effort to teach themselves, then I'll suggest that this should be their first priority. I strongly believe people should make the effort to self-learn before being considered for a training course because it'll be far more effective for both them and the organization. Of course, there will be times when you'll need to send someone for training because their job requires it. However, if you spend time with them before they start, to explain why this training is so important for them and their career (and not just for the company), then they should be more motivated to get the most value out of it.

Enhancing performance through coaching

Coaching centres on helping an individual think through problems and apply knowledge they already have in a more effective way. A good coach is someone for the employee to learn with, not from. Coaches rarely offer the solution; instead, they simply guide, helping the individual to think for themselves. You may have had employees or colleagues who ask for your help and expect you to give them the solution when in fact they just need encouragement to figure it out. Helping them to consider all the options so that they solve the problem on their own will deliver a deeper learning experience than just fixing it for them.

Coaching is an intrinsic part of your role as manager. You know your team's purpose and what's required of it; you know the individuals, their strengths and their capability gaps; you'll have an existing relationship with them that means they (hopefully) trust and respect you; and you'll already know where they might be struggling. You're an ideal person to help guide your employees to meet the challenges and situations they face. If you aspire to be the best manager, then developing great coaching skills will really help you to continuously develop your employees.

A great coaching experience is a marriage between questions that stimulate thinking and conscious listening that allows each question to build on the answer to the last one. Importantly, coaching is not about telling or advising, which is what sets it apart from feedback and training.

Good coaching questions are thought provoking, invite reflection, expand possibilities, bring underlying assumptions to light, stimulate creativity and are outcome focused. They will likely fall into one of six broad categories, depending on the objective of the coaching session:

- **Investigative:** When you want to explore a specific situation, e.g. 'Why do you think that happened?'

- **Drawing out:** To probe deeper in order to discover an underlying issue, e.g. 'Why do you think that's important?'

- **Catalytic:** When the employee needs stimulation to consider a different point of view, e.g. 'What other approaches could you take?'

- **Big picture:** When there's a need to appreciate the wider impact of a decision or action, e.g. 'What might be the consequences of doing that?'

- **Strategic:** For exploring the consequences of one choice over another, e.g. 'What do you think are the benefits of option A over option B?'

- **Pre-emptive:** Helping the employee to consider possible implications, challenges, or actions taken by others, e.g. 'How do you think they might react if you did that?'

There are a number of frameworks you can use to structure and bring focus to a coaching session with an employee. Each differs in terminology, but most follow the same general approach. When a team member approaches you and asks for your help regarding a particular issue, structure your discussion in this order:

1 **Topic:** What is the specific problem they want to solve, the outcome they wish to reach or the decision they need to make?

2 **Context:** Why is this an issue for them right now? What progress has the employee made so far? What's holding them back from making further progress? For the coach, this stage is about listening and asking catalytic questions to get to the crux of the issue that needs to be addressed. Many times I've found an employee's request for help on a task is less to do with their ability to execute and more about their doubts about their own capabilities or willingness to take a risk. Try asking questions like 'Why don't you feel able to make this decision yourself?'

3 **Options:** Draw out what the employee could do to address the issue. This stage is not about offering advice but rather helping the employee think through the options and choices open to them. Questions like 'What else could you do?' followed by the repetition of 'What else?' are great for stimulating ideas and forcing the employee to brainstorm additional potential solutions beyond their initial assumptions.

4 **Priorities:** Once you have helped the employee to develop a list of options, encourage them to choose or prioritize the ones they'll action. It's important that the employee makes these decisions, not you, so they retain ownership and accountability.

Finish the session by encouraging the employee to summarize what they will do and getting them to make a verbal commitment to a deadline. If appropriate, and if the person agrees, schedule follow-up appointments to review progress towards the goal and help them adjust their path if necessary.

Coaching is a skill and a tool you can deploy at any time. It doesn't always require a dedicated meeting. Whenever someone asks for your advice, try to respond as a coach rather than a teacher. As their manager, it'll be very tempting to just tell them what to do. Instead, by answering with a question like 'What options have you considered?' you'll encourage the employee to think for themselves. You'll often find your employees just want to delegate responsibility for the decision to you. Resist and let them make their own choices. Even if you think they haven't quite nailed it, empowering them through autonomy will provide a motivational energy shot.

Mentoring others

It's likely that you have reached the position you're in now because you've excelled in your chosen discipline. That should make you an excellent mentor to others who are behind you in their career trajectory. Mentors help others by sharing their own experience of a job, industry, organization or culture in order to provide inspiration, boost confidence and help their mentee make better decisions and progress faster. Mentoring is particularly important to people from minority groups who may have experienced structural barriers to success, or a lack of access to role models in senior leadership positions. Even CEOs have mentors: other senior executives with more experience from whom they can learn.

Unlike coaching, mentoring does involve the sharing of advice. At one extreme it can be very instructional, with a focus on specific knowledge transfer that will help the individual perform in their current role. At the other extreme it can be more developmental, where guiding and supporting the mentee's broader long-term development, particularly with regard to career progression, is the primary engagement. It can also take different forms:

- **One-to-one mentoring:** When an experienced individual mentors someone less accomplished.

- **Peer-to-peer mentoring:** The pairing up of two people at a similar level to support each other.

- **Group mentoring:** Bringing together multiple people with similar learning interests or needs, such as a study group at college.

- **Reverse mentoring:** When a younger individual mentors a more senior person, often to share insight into what life is like today for those in younger demographics.

The critical components of an effective mentoring relationship are trust, candid and confidential communication, and a clear understanding of its scope and objectives from the start. In your first meeting with a mentee, I recommend you create clarity around the exact scope of your relationship to keep the discussions focused on the individual's objectives and avoid any ambiguities and tangents. For example:

- What help are they seeking?

- Why do they feel you're the best person to help them with their goals?

- How do they want to benefit from your experience?

- How much time do they (and you) want to commit to the mentoring?

- What does success look like for them?

I've found the most common request for a mentor is to facilitate career development. Many young people aren't able to articulate a career plan because they don't know all the options that are available to them. As a mentor, you'll be able to deliver huge value to an individual by simply helping them understand the paths open to them or more clearly articulating what they actually want to achieve in life, which might be different from what they *think* they want. Mentoring is also a great way to reset unrealistic expectations. Sharing the reality of life in their chosen profession is an important part of this, especially for those who may have a sense of entitlement.

How to support your superstar employees

While you should care about the development of all your employees, the reality is that intellectual, emotional and physical capabilities vary. Just as it is hard to turn a weakness into a strength, it takes effort to turn an average employee into a superstar. That's not to say you shouldn't try. Coaching has been shown to produce miraculous results simply by stimulating a change in attitude, motivation or self-belief. Individuals who lack confidence, or who feel they have been held back through discrimination or blocked opportunities, can be transformed when given the chance and a bit of encouragement. However, you shouldn't expect everyone to be a top performer. The reality is that your efforts to improve through personal development will have more impact on some than on others.

Most organizations form lists of high-potential employees – individuals they have singled out for extra development because the return on investment will be greatest. Whether you are managing a large department or just a small team of two or three, spotting your future superstars can help you to prioritize your time and budget in favour of those likely to benefit most. The important consideration here is that these individuals offer high *potential*. They may not necessarily be your strongest performers today, but the way they operate suggests they could become your greatest contributors in the future with some additional help.

What are the signals that can identify these high potentials? In the same way that the best managers tend to exhibit similar behaviours, individuals who are regarded as high performers by their employers, across many different types of organization, also conduct themselves in remarkably similar ways. That's not to say high performers are all the same, but there is consistency in their attitudes and how they behave that aligns with the delivery of strong results. These signals are especially important when hiring people for your team. Since you'll generally only have circumstantial evidence around a candidate's past performance, you'll need to make a recruitment decision based on whether you think they have the potential to do well in the future.

The traits that are most common among high-performing individuals are:

1 **Intrinsic motivation:** A strong internal source of energy to push themselves to achieve hard things.

2 **Emotional intelligence:** The ability to communicate with others in a sensitive and respectful way, while appreciating how they might be feeling.

3 **Initiative:** The ability to see what needs to be done, to bring solutions not problems, and proactively make things happen.

4 **Grit:** Perseverance in the face of adversity, with an ability to overcome barriers as they arise.

5 **Curiosity:** A natural inquisitiveness to learn new skills, build knowledge and solve problems.

6 **Collaboration:** An ability to work effectively with others, both accepting and offering help.

7 **Communication:** The ability to communicate concisely, with clarity, and actively listen to others.

8 **Self-management:** The organizational skills required to work independently without relying heavily on others for structure and direction.

9 **Values:** A clear sense of right and wrong.

10 **History of achievement:** A history of exceeding expectations, receiving awards or being promoted.

You can learn new skills, but it's harder to learn a new attitude. In interviews, or when I'm considering someone for promotion or targeted development, I always look for evidence of motivation, emotional intelligence, initiative, grit and curiosity as the strongest indicators of future potential. Only if they tick those boxes do I consider whether they have the functional skills and experience to do the job required. When you're reviewing your team, the ten traits listed will help you to spot the individuals most likely to achieve great things for you in the future.

Motivate first, then develop

Even highly talented employees will struggle to do a good job for you if they lack the motivation to do so. A focus on development without also ensuring each team member is engaged in their work will create frustration and disappointment. Motivation must come first – without this, they just won't care.

But employees don't operate in isolation. They, and you, are part of a team, and every group of people has its own dynamic that can ratchet up performance or create a toxic working environment that holds everyone back. In the next chapter we'll explore the importance of culture and what you can do to create the ideal working environment for a high-performing team.

Chapter takeaways

- Capability development is how you actually improve an employee's performance.

- Feedback lets an employee know how they're doing and should comprise praise and recognition more often than criticism.

- When letting an employee know they haven't met your expectations, remain objective and use facts and behavioural examples to avoid your comments being regarded as solely an opinion. Structure your discussion with COIN: Context, Observation, Impact, Next steps.

- Emotional reactions are often due to misinterpretation or misunderstanding. You can rescue emotional situations by focusing on what was actually said or done and the real intent behind it.

- Training makes people capable by giving them the skills or experience they need to do their job effectively. It is most effective when the participant is motivated to learn.

- Coaching is a great method of instilling a sense of autonomy in your employees because it helps them to solve problems by applying knowledge they already have in new ways. To become a great coach, you'll need to avoid the temptation to tell and instead learn how to question.

- Mentoring allows others to learn and be inspired by your own experience and is especially valuable for those in minority or disadvantaged groups.

- The highest-performing employees tend to exhibit common behaviours and attitudes. You can use these to identify those in your team who are most likely to become your strongest employees in the future.

Step 4: Build a High-Performance Culture

Why culture matters

Between 2012 and 2015, Google's People Operations team ran a company-wide research project to investigate why its highest-performing teams were so much more effective than others. Google analysed more than 250 attributes of over 180 different teams across the company with the goal of understanding what set the best teams apart from the rest. This project put to bed the assumption that a group of highly talented individuals would always make a high-performing team. A laser focus on simply maximizing each employee's individual contribution simply creates an organization of lone wolves who fail to appreciate how their work needs to support and feed off the work of others. Instead, Google's research concluded that *who* is on a team matters far less than *how* the team members work together.[1]

How people work together is underpinned by the culture of the team or organization. Culture is not the carefully crafted mission statements and lists of company values you often see adorning the walls of corporate reception areas. It is something you observe and experience through the behaviours of the people who exist within the organization. Your team's culture is a collection of its 'group norms': the behavioural standards and unwritten rules that govern how your employees function together. These norms can be either unspoken or openly acknowledged, but their influence is significant because when people gather it is these norms of accepted behaviour that usually override individual propensities. When everyone in a group behaves in ways that align with these collective group norms, everyone feels relaxed and energized. But when someone's behaviour runs counter to a group's norms, everyone is put on guard. The outsider is perceived as a threat to the established order. It's one reason why the first few weeks working for a new employer are so stressful: you have to figure out what these norms of behaviour are by observing others, while not putting your foot in it by breaking the unwritten rules that others regard as sacrosanct. When recruiters talk about cultural fit, what they really mean is 'Will the candidate be comfortable operating under the existing group norms in the team?' Culture is crucial to the effective functioning of your team; you should become obsessed by it.

Left uncontrolled, group norms can become a powerful constraint on your ability to get results as a manager because they act as a force against change. With active intent, however, you can harness them as a source of additional energy to multiply the effectiveness of each individual in your team. While you may not be able to influence your organization's culture as a whole, there are strategies you can follow that will enable you to influence the culture within your team. Organizational culture is set by the worst behaviour you tolerate, so it's essential you live by the standards you expect yourself and understand which unattractive group behaviours you'll need to stamp out. In this chapter, we'll explore how you can influence not only how people work but also how they work together.

The six qualities of high-performing teams

As with the qualities of high-performing managers, much has been written about what makes a team highly effective. Google has studied it extensively; top management consultancies have researched it (and claimed the results as their own unique secret methodology); many university academics have published their own theories. Each study produced different results, but their conclusions regarding what makes a team operate in a highly effective way are all similar and can be summarized into six qualities:

1 Psychological safety.

2 Purpose.

3 Belonging.

4 Trust.

5 Energy.

6 Impact.

Let's explore each one in detail.

Psychological safety

This is the overarching set of group norms that makes your team a safe space in which each individual can work in their own authentic way. It lays an essential foundation for creating group affiliation. Psychological safety provides confidence that the team will not embarrass, reject or punish you for making mistakes, speaking up or sharing a controversial point of view. It is the mutual respect that allows individuals to be comfortable being themselves. Energy is focused around creativity, problem solving and divergent thinking, rather than defensiveness and finger-pointing. Opinions can be freely expressed, direct feedback can be given and failure regarded as an acceptable consequence of exploring new ideas.

While a feeling of affiliation to the group can depend upon the relationships your employees have with each other, creating a psychologically safe team environment is entirely within your control. It's up to you, explicitly through your words and implicitly through your behaviours, to let everyone know what the rules are that you expect everyone to live by. Here are a few ways in which you can communicate to your team that it is a safe space for them to be themselves:

Define your values

Explicitly involve your team in defining the group norms and values that you all want to live by. You'll find the ideas that are volunteered will be those that make each person comfortable within your team environment.

Ensure everyone's opinion is heard

Tell your team that each person's opinion matters and encourage everyone to participate in discussions so that their points of view are considered equally. It's often the quietest employees who make the best contributions because they're the ones who think before they speak, but they might need to be invited into the debate. In your meetings, spot the people who haven't contributed and ask for their opinion on what's being discussed.

Avoid using the word 'but' in response to someone's suggestion (as in, 'Thanks for that idea, but . . .')

This is a rejection word and it signals you're dismissing the other person's comment out of hand without any real consideration. Instead of passing your own judgement, solicit further opinions – as in, 'Thanks for that idea; what does everyone else think of it?'

Give due consideration to controversial ideas

Ideas that run counter to the existing orthodoxy may still offer a valid and valuable contribution to any debate. Don't dismiss anyone's contribution without good reason.

Be clear, honest and direct

Ambiguous feedback that doesn't clearly deliver the intended message won't have an impact. Let everyone know that you'll be giving them direct feedback, that you want them to feel comfortable with this and that they are free to give you a candid response.

Allow failure to be an acceptable consequence of exploring new ideas

Failure and success are seen as opposites, but in reality, failing is part of succeeding. Growth requires creativity and innovation, but experimentation doesn't always deliver a successful outcome. If you're not failing, you're not innovating. Unfortunately, the law of loss aversion – that the pain of losses is approximately double the joy of gains – means that in many companies, creating a large gain will lead to modest recognition and reward, while even a moderate failure could destroy your career. Consequently, organizations naturally become highly risk averse. Punishing mistakes and failures in your team will shut down creativity and ensure the status quo prevails. To establish a growth culture, you'll need to prove to your employees that you accept mistakes as an inevitable result of them trying out new ideas. Recognize people for trying, even if the result isn't what was hoped. If you deconstruct unsuccessful initiatives, the group can learn collectively from the mistakes of others. Acknowledging that things rarely work perfectly will create a safety net that will help your growth culture to flourish.

Deal quickly with unacceptable behaviour

Psychological safety will rapidly break down if some people get away with behaviours that undermine the group norms others abide by. Cultures quickly become toxic when individuals disengage from the team and others begin replicating the bad behaviours they see others exhibiting. Deal with these situations quickly and visibly to demonstrate that you are serious and use this action to reinforce the behaviours and attitudes you want to encourage.

Actively promote diversity

Diverse teams are smarter, more creative and make better business decisions than uniform ones because their members bring differing points of view to discussions. Creating an environment that is inclusive to everyone and ensuring that all voices have equal weight and opportunity is key to running a successful team.

Share your own vulnerabilities

An easy way to build trust and openness in a team is to share your personal sensitivities and vulnerabilities. As the manager, be the first at volunteering some insights into your own personality, anxieties and worries. Such openness from the boss will encourage others to reveal their own concerns and issues. This deeper level of interpersonal connection among your team will help each member to become more authentic and empathetic.

Of the six high-performing team indicators, all the research in this area identifies psychological safety as by far the most important and influential in determining team performance. This is the one to ensure you get right; all the others stem from it and feed off it. A failure to establish a feeling of security in your team will make it harder to create a sense of belonging and maintain the open dialogue necessary for each person to work at their best.

Purpose

As we saw in Step 1, purpose is all about the *why*. Why are we doing this and why does it matter? Purpose powers team effectiveness because each member feels they are working to deliver something that is personally important, and they understand the contribution they must each make to help the team achieve its objective. Unless the whole team understands and buys into the impact it needs to deliver, there will always be one or more dissenting members holding the group back, intentionally or not. A common sense of purpose underpins each individual's personal motivation.

When communicating the *why*, organizational leaders typically tell two types of stories to inspire their teams. The first focuses on why the business needs to change or improve: 'We need to improve the quality of our service because our competitors are taking market share.' The second focuses on how great the company could be if only people worked harder: 'We have so much potential and opportunity if we get this right.'

Both of these approaches centre on the benefits to the company, which is naturally what's most important for business executives. However, research by management consultancy firm McKinsey,[2] along with my own experience, suggests that you're likely to inspire greater motivation among your employees using messages that are focused on how their work impacts people rather than the organization. For example, try telling stories based on the impact of each employee's work on:

- **Customers:** How it makes people's lives easier, more enjoyable, less expensive or more rewarding.

- **Colleagues:** How it assists co-workers to achieve their own objectives by enabling them to be more effective in what they do.

- **Themselves:** How it supports personal growth or career advancement.

- **Society:** How their work helps to build a better community, assists those in need, benefits the environment or facilitates social cohesion.

What's the best way to instil a common and collective sense of meaning into your team? Tell stories. In particular, tell stories based on how your team's work, and each individual's contribution to it, affects other people. Repeatedly remind your employees why their work is important to others, for example, 'We need to improve the quality of our service because our customers deserve the best and they're telling us they're not satisfied.'

Belonging

True team cohesion requires every member to have a sense of affiliation to the group. This doesn't mean everyone has to like each other (although that obviously helps). Belonging to a group just requires individuals to feel a common bond with their colleagues so that they believe they're accepted by others as an insider rather than outsider.

You can increase your employees' sense of belonging to the team by establishing:

- **Inclusion:** Individuals show respect for others and their views, even if these diverge from their own. Diversity is embraced and encouraged.

- **Openness:** Honest, open, transparent dialogue helps to create mutual respect, recognition and empathy among team members.

- **Dependability:** Team members feel able to rely on their colleagues to produce high-quality work in a timely manner, and to highlight potential delays at an early stage so that disruption to others can be managed. Work that's delegated will be done as required and individuals can be trusted to do what others are expecting of them, even when they're not being supervised.

- **Rules:** Group norms align with each individual's beliefs and attitudes so that each person is confident others will behave as they themselves would behave. These norms are agreed, understood and followed by everyone in the team.

- **Personal connections:** Personal relationships rarely arise from attending meetings. Interactions that nurture deeper relationships are those that happen away from the desk. Team bonding activities away from the office really do help because they peel away individuals' workplace façades and create an environment where conversations don't need to be about the office, where people can relax and feel comfortable opening up about their interests, vulnerabilities and unique quirks. I use Friday afternoon drinks and occasional group lunches or dinners to help me get to know my team, and for them to bond with each other.

Facilitating relationships is only part of your responsibility as a manager here. You'll also need proactively to encourage the behaviours which demonstrate that inclusion, openness and dependability are part of your team's culture. Ensure each person knows that unreliability is unacceptable, stamp out disrespect and celebrate everyone's unique personalities, interests and life preferences.

Trust

Trust is the foundation on which all relationships are built. It is that deeper bond which means you place faith in others' decisions and not just their actions. Trust arises when you have a common understanding of each other's motivations, ambitions, weaknesses and unique talents. When you depend on others, trust gives you the confidence they will do what you expect. In a team with high levels of trust, you know everyone is doing the right thing for the right reasons, even when no one is watching. A team that lacks trust assumes everyone acts in their own selfish interests, and this gives permission for each individual to make decisions based on what's best for them, not what's right for the team. Without respect, there's no trust. Without trust, there's no relationship. Without relationships, there's no team.

As well as establishing trust among your employees, you'll need to convince them that they can trust you. You'll only be granted permission to give negative feedback if they trust you since otherwise they won't accept what you say. Trust is hard to create artificially – you'll need to prove, not just say, that you are as good as your word. You'll have to earn your team's trust over time by adhering to the rules and behaviours you expect them to abide by, such as:

- Authentic and consistent behaviour.

- Consideration and compassion.

- Honesty and integrity.

- Reliability and dependability.

- Empathy and emotional control.

- Openness and transparency.

- Recognition of good work and genuine effort.

While trust is earned over time, it can be destroyed in an instant. You cannot let your team's trust in you – what you say and the decisions you make – be tarnished. Your employees will ignore the million things you do well while focusing on the one thing you get wrong. So don't make easily avoidable mistakes, such as saying one thing but doing another. We'll explore more of these communication pitfalls in Step 5: 'Master Your Communication'.

Energy

Left to themselves, living systems lose energy over time. Things slow down, momentum declines, commitment wanes. Self-motivation consumes a huge amount of energy, which is why we're so committed to new initiatives like a gym membership or a diet at the beginning but find these become a real struggle later on. To reinject energy, we often have to rely on others to keep us moving forward. We supplement the gym membership with a personal trainer to keep us motivated to exercise; we join a diet group whose weekly weigh-ins motivate us to keep temptation at bay.

In the same way, a team also needs a continual reinjection of motivating energy to maintain its performance. As a manager, you'll need to set the context that will help your team members find their inner incentives and generate the sparks that will keep them firing, especially during periods when self-motivation becomes difficult.

Energy can be injected in many ways. If you've had the sensation that energy levels are low among the members of your team, that's exactly when you need to take responsibility for reinvigorating them. Besides the obvious need for individuals to be well fed and rested, try these eight methods for raising energy levels:

Give the office a facelift

The physical space in which you work can boost or drain energy levels. Natural light, plants and bright colours can lift spirits, while blandness and windowless rooms sap everyone's drive. Background music really helps sustain energy levels, especially in offices where there is little chatter. Providing a change of surroundings – by taking everyone off-site, for example – can top up energy levels.

Mix things up

If you manage a team where everyone mostly does the same thing every day, or they've been working on the same project for a while, give people something different to do. Assign them an interesting side project to work on or swap responsibilities.

Rally the team behind a charitable cause

Providing help to others is a great way to recharge your team's battery. That uplifting feeling you get when others show genuine gratitude for support you've given is the energy flowing back into your reserves. Charitable causes are especially powerful at re-energizing a team. As well as making a difference to someone else's life or the local environment, the experience of coming together for a good cause can deepen the interpersonal bonds between your team members.

Be energetic, exciting and passion-filled

Simply exuding energy yourself will make a huge impact on your team. You don't need to run around the office like a four-year-old; just bringing some passion, intonation, volume and spark to your voice can be sufficient.

Celebrate successes

Show people how much progress has been made by highlighting successes, no matter how small. Stories can be especially energizing if they focus on impassioned motivations, such as when a customer provides a really uplifting review.

Give recognition

A pat on the back or shout out in a team meeting to celebrate great work delivers a huge volume of motivational calories at zero cost.

Provide autonomy

As we've discussed earlier, giving people the freedom to do work in the way they want to can supercharge their feeling of empowerment, one of the most powerful drivers of intrinsic energy.

Help individuals find their potential and purpose

Give your team a clearer purpose by reminding them why their work matters and helping them get into their flow by allowing them to do work they love and want to be great at.

While you try to boost energy levels, also think about what might be sapping energy from the group. Meandering meetings, unnecessary bureaucracy, over-blunt feedback, lack of recognition and support, ineffective technology – these are all energy sinkholes. Take a moment to think about what you might do subconsciously that could sap the energy of others, and consider running your own 'Bureaucracy Buster' sessions to identify unnecessary inefficiencies that wear your team down.

Impact

Ultimately, the output a team generates is its entire reason for existing. A team that works hard without generating any meaningful impact would hardly be regarded as high performing. Sometimes this quality is referred to as 'results' or 'output'.

However, I prefer to use 'impact' because it emphasizes the need for your output to make an actual difference. Output without impact is just people being busy but achieving little.

In this context, your team's impact doesn't just refer to the final output of its collective work; it's more about having an always-on attention to results. It begins with having a clear set of expectations defined for everyone up front and prioritizing activities so that the things that must be done well have sufficient resources invested in them to succeed. It's about measuring progress and plotting course changes rapidly if things aren't working out. It's about people taking personal responsibility for making things happen. In the most effective teams, everyone takes ownership of results and accepts accountability for delivering them.

I've found a common reason for team underperformance is simply a lack of attention to results. People find ways to fill their days so they feel busy, but they may not be focused on delivering the right outputs. Consequently, the best way to keep your team focused on its impact is to invest time in creating structure, clarity and measurement mechanisms around each person's objectives and KPIs. A team's impact is simply an aggregation of each individual's contribution; keeping each person focused on what you expect them to deliver and closely monitoring their progress will help you to establish an impact-orientated culture.

The group norms that lead to dysfunctional teams

Establishing a high-performance team through the positive mechanisms described above needs to be accompanied by the elimination of established group norms that may act as a constraint on performance. This is particularly important if you're taking on a set of employees who may have existing ways of working that will conflict with what you now know will maximize their performance.

Take a moment to reflect on teams you have been part of in the past. Have they always operated smoothly? Which teams seemed to gel and which were dysfunctional? What tensions existed that might have put a brake on effective collaboration? Here are some of the most common norms of poor team behaviour you should look out for and take active measures to eradicate:

Communication and collaboration issues

- **Silos:** Teams that splinter into smaller factions can reduce their diversity of thought and collaboration.

- **Disorderly discussions:** As any chairperson knows, effective debate requires everyone's voice to be heard and consideration given to each speaker's contribution. Discussions driven by argument, interruption, side-comments, distractions, put-downs or silence rarely deliver an optimal result.

- **Groupthink:** The team becomes comfortable with the established way of looking at problems and fails to explore alternative perspectives.

- **Avoiding disagreement:** Individuals too readily accept the ideas of others without due thought, discussion or debate.

- **Gossip:** While it's always entertaining to know what's happening behind the scenes, gossip is rarely positive. It seeds rumours, hardens negative perceptions, reduces respect and erects interpersonal barriers where none existed.

- **Finger-pointing:** When team members begin to assign blame, individuals become defensive and reluctant to take responsibility for making decisions. It's a sign of low trust and safety in the team.

Ineffective processes

- **Lack of decision-making:** An inability to form sufficient consensus to make a decision is indicative of a lack of debate, respect and trust in others. The absence of decisions results in teams failing to move forward.

- **Unilateral decision-making:** The opposite of too little decision-making happens when one team member takes it upon themselves to make all the decisions without establishing the appropriate authority from the others to do this.

- **Workload imbalance:** Individuals naturally work at different paces, but when one or two individuals end up carrying the bulk of the workload then resentment sets in.

- **Fixation on problems, not solutions:** It's easy to spot things that aren't working well, so teams can become fixated on problems without recognizing and celebrating what's succeeding. A culture of complaint distracts the team from trying to find solutions to the problems.

As the manager, it'll be up to you to spot and address any of the issues listed above that might exist among your employees by indicating that these habits and attitudes are unacceptable and ensuring no new ones become established. Failing to deal with these issues quickly will hold back your attempts to instil a more positive culture based around psychological safety, belonging and trust.

How to instil a new culture

Unfortunately, you can't change a culture overnight. While you can do much to establish a sense of psychological safety and trust yourself, a culture lives and breathes through all its members and it will take time for each member of your team to adapt, shed any barriers they might have erected and develop new bonds with their colleagues. Here are a few additional tips to help you accelerate this process:

Explain why things need to change

Humans inherently don't like change. It's far easier to just continue with old habits. To overcome this inertia, you'll need to provide a push to each team member. As we learnt earlier in this book, the most powerful motivations are intrinsic, so the best way to instigate change is to make every employee want it. Analyse the bad habits and negative group norms you've observed and identify the reasons these are holding back each person's performance. Ask your team what they think is wrong with the team culture and what they would want to change. Then paint a picture of how much more productive, energized, happy and authentic they could be in the new future you want to create. Make them excited about what their working day will be like in this new team environment.

Document your new culture's core facets

While many group norms are unwritten and can be observed only through the way people behave, it is still a good idea to write down the ones most crucial to the success of your team. If you're expecting individuals to adapt to new ways of working, you'll need to define clearly how you now want everyone to operate. It's also easier for new team members to adhere to the group's norms if they are written down. Documenting the core facets of your new culture, such as in a code of conduct, will help everyone to understand what's acceptable and what is not.

When I inherit a new team or business, I share with every employee a simple document, no more than one page, that describes the core philosophies I follow and would like them to adopt. I've found this document to be priceless because it allows others to understand how I work as a manager and identify what's going to be different compared with how they've been managed in the past. I also share the document with every new starter to accelerate their understanding and adoption of the group norms they will be expected to work under. If you'd like to see what's included in my code of conduct, you can download it from www.managingpeople.tips.

You'll need to decide what you want the group norms to be for your team. It'll depend on what's resonated with you in this book, the type of organization you're in and its existing culture, and the management style you choose to adopt. I recommend you consider including some or all of these guidelines:

- **Meeting etiquette:** Arrive on time, remain disconnected from phones and email, speak frankly, succinctly and courteously and ensure clear actions are agreed, understood and accepted.

- **Flexible working/office hours:** Work when and where you are most productive. The main thing is that the work you're expected to deliver gets done to the best of your ability.

- **Receiving and giving feedback:** Everyone should feel comfortable offering feedback to anyone else, at any time. Expect feedback to be direct, candid, honest and timely, and intended to help the other person to do even better. Follow this approach when offering feedback to others.

- **Prioritization:** It's OK to say no to any request if there is a justifiable reason, such as not compromising existing commitments. It's also OK to change priorities if warranted.

- **Disagree and commit:** The appropriate time to express disagreement is during the debate, but once a decision has been made, accept it and commit to doing what has been agreed.

- **Acknowledge mistakes:** Mistakes are a necessary result of experimentation, but each mistake should only be made once.

- **Dependability:** If you agree to a deadline, others will assume you've committed to it and will be relying upon you to achieve it. So always deliver what you say you will, and if you can't, let the team know in advance.

Expect everyone to adhere to high standards

Setting high standards and aspiring to meet them is unrelated to intellect, experience or talent. Even graduates fresh out of college with no experience can adopt and exhibit high standards. The key here is that everyone needs to know what those standards are and that they are expected to adhere to them. Jeff Bezos, founder of global e-commerce giant Amazon, neatly summarized how you should think about this:[3]

High standards are contagious

Create an environment where high standards are the norm and you'll find they become contagious simply through exposure. Bring a new person into a high-standard team and they will quickly adapt their behaviours and ambitions to fit this culture.

High standards need to be recognized to be understood

It's easy to recognize high standards when you see them, but you have to experience them yourself to understand fully where the bar lies. As the manager, it'll be your job to live and breathe these standards through your own behaviours. You'll need to be comfortable telling people they haven't exceeded the bar you've set and pushing them to stretch higher.

Everyone can always deliver better quality work

In an infamous anecdote, Bezos is presented with a report and asks the writer whether this is the best they can do. Taking this as an indication Bezos isn't happy with it, the writer then sheepishly withdraws, updates and resubmits the report. Once again, Bezos asks if this is the best they can do. The writer goes away and further enhances the report. Finally, when asked if this is now his best work, the writer answers that it is. Bezos then admits that now he's actually going to read it. While it is important to recognize when time constraints require you to take a 'good enough' approach, an adherence to high standards should require you to push your team to improve work they think is already their best.

You don't need to be an expert yourself

As the team's leader, you don't need to be skilled yourself in all the knowledge areas your team encompasses. Setting high standards should be based on the output you want to achieve. How your team achieves these is up to them to figure out. You just need to know enough about the job to be able to set expectations that are appropriate and achievable, while recognizing great work when you see it.

Don't expect everyone to be a high performer

Although you should set high standards and expect everyone to deliver good-quality work, a high-performing team doesn't require every team member to be a high performer. After all, the most successful sports teams usually have only two or three star players; the rest of the team exists to support and enable their success. The contribution your team makes will be determined more by how your employees work together than by individual intellect and ambition. In fact, a team comprising only high performers may actually underperform as each person jockeys for the limelight, pushing for their own views to hold sway. Instead, try to recognize everyone's unique role within your team by mentally placing each person into one of these four groups:

- **Superheroes:** The individuals who have the ambition, intrinsic motivation, intellect and talent to be the engine that drives innovation and growth. These employees instinctively see what needs to be done, and do it quickly and well. They energize and excite others and demonstrate natural leadership, no matter where they sit in the organizational hierarchy. They are your team's engine.

- **Rock stars:** These are the trusted workers who can be relied upon to do their job well. They are the crankshaft that transmits the power of your team's engine to the wheels.

- **Roadies:** These individuals work tirelessly behind the scenes to support everyone else by reliably doing the work that others aren't motivated by. They handle the repetitive, administrative tasks that need to be done well for the team's service promise to be upheld. They are the wheels that keep the team headed in the right direction.

- **Fans:** These are the individuals who sit off to the side and only dip in and out of your team occasionally to provide input and guidance. Fans might be the sales reps who take your team's products to market. They are the ones who are best placed to critique what your team does because they aren't deeply involved in its day-to-day work and can assess the finished product in relation to what they were expecting.

Roadies have a clear and very valuable role in your team as they do the grunt work nobody else is willing to do – just don't expect them to become your rock stars or superheroes. A high-performing team just needs each person to do their specific job well; it doesn't require everyone to be a headline act.

Work to harness strengths, not fix weaknesses

As a new manager, you can disregard the philosophy that's so ingrained in the learning and development departments of large corporations: that personal development plans should focus on improving weaknesses. It's rare that anyone can 'fix' a weakness and turn it into a strength. You might be able to make a weakness less weak, but without an enormous amount of effort and personality change it's very unlikely ever to become a strength. Life is too short to spend all our time working on things we're not very good at. We won't enjoy it, and if work isn't enjoyable then our intrinsic motivation will evaporate.

Instead, play to each individual's strengths. Determine what each person is really good at (their 'native genius') or loves doing (their 'passion') and build on these by finding roles for them within the team that will allow them to use their strengths to the full. Help people to get into their flow and you'll be amazed by the results they achieve.

This is not to say that you should ignore weaknesses. Clearly, if an individual isn't effective at a core competence required for the role then that will need to be addressed. However, it may also indicate that they're simply in the wrong job. A critical look at what they are good at and genuinely interested in might reveal other career paths they would be better suited to.

Remember, most people don't know what their strengths are until someone tells them. The things employees say they are good at often do not match up with what their managers observe as their strengths. Things we are good at seem easy; consequently, we may not appreciate that these activities are hard for other people. As a manager, it's vitally important to let each person in your team know what you regard as their strengths. Observe how each person works, identify what each does that's superior to others, then tell them what these natural talents are.

Communicate clearly and often

It may sound obvious, but changing a culture requires leadership. You'll need to adhere to even higher standards than those you're expecting of your team. Any lapse in your own behaviour, by turning up late to meetings or showing yourself to be untrustworthy, for example, will severely undermine your ability to establish the new group norms you expect others to adopt.

It will also require strong and inspiring communication. You'll need to be clear about what needs to change and why. You'll need to motivate a desire to change by painting a picture of how much better things will be for everyone in the new future. You'll need to deal with those who remain resistant to the new ways of working while being sympathetic to their concerns and open to other ideas. And, importantly, you'll need to listen to their feedback so that the new culture is born from within and not imposed from above. That's why the fifth and final pillar in our framework for becoming a great manager is communication. In the next chapter I'll share tips on how to improve the way you deliver messages so that they are believed, understood, remembered and actioned.

....

Chapter takeaways

- When considering how to improve a team's performance, *who* is on the team matters far less than *how* the team members work together.

- Group norms are the behavioural standards and unwritten rules that govern how your employees function as a team. To promote a high-performance culture, you'll need to instil positive group norms that contribute to productive, effective collaboration and stamp out negative group norms that hold everyone back.

- The six qualities common to most high-performing teams are: psychological safety, purpose, belonging, trust, energy and impact. Of these, psychological safety is by far the most important and influential factor that underpins the highest-performing teams.

- To migrate towards a better culture, you'll need to explain to your team why change is needed and what you want to change, then motivate them to want to change by showing them how much better life will be for them in the new future.

Step 5: Master Your Communication

Communication underpins everything else

Your ability to communicate effectively creates the foundations for everything else you do as a manager. It is at the heart of how you'll build relationships, motivate people and stimulate engagement. It is how your team will know what to do, why they need to do it and how well they're doing. It is through the way you communicate that you build influence, trust and credibility. When communication breaks down, so do productivity and morale. While great storytelling will inspire and motivate, confused messaging will hold back both your success as a manager and the effectiveness of your team. Communication is one of the most essential skills to master, yet it is also the skill that many newly appointed managers struggle with the most.

In this chapter we'll explore why what you say may not be what other people hear, the steps you can take to ensure your messages are understood as you intend, and how you can employ active listening techniques to correctly interpret the messages that others are consciously and unconsciously communicating to you.

Communication is about being understood

Becoming a strong leader requires becoming a powerful story-teller. Stories capture the imagination, explain complicated issues in simple ways and engage an audience with your vision. However, it's easy to assume that communication is just what we say to each other, in either spoken or written form. Under this preset, becoming an effective communicator requires only a mastery of words. But communication always has a purpose. Every time we speak there's an intention to create a reaction. We want our audience to do something, gain an understanding or feel some form of emotion, such as laughter, happiness, excitement or sadness. Communication without a reaction is like speaking to an empty hall – you're sending a message but nobody's listening. Truly effective communication happens only when our message is heard, interpreted as we intended, understood, remembered and actioned as we want it to be. As George Bernard Shaw once said, 'The greatest problem in communication is the illusion that it has been accomplished.'

Communication is not about the words you say; it is about the message that is received and the reaction it causes in the listener, both of which rely on interpretation. Too often we think we've delivered a message without actually checking if it was understood as we intended. These misunderstandings are a very common cause of confusion, frustration and wasted effort in teams.

Misunderstandings often arise through tone. Tone is *how* you say something. It is the quality in your voice that expresses your inner feelings or thoughts, such as sympathy, anger, interest, humility, shock or urgency. Very often it is not the words that cause a message to be misinterpreted but rather the tone of voice in which it is delivered. Can you think of a time when someone made a comment to you that sounded patronizing? Did they intend to patronize you? Probably not, but their inappropriate tone may have left you with that impression. The reason you know someone is in a bad mood is because their tone frames your entire conversation with them.

What are the other ways a message might fail to be interpreted as we expected? To understand this requires exploration of all the ways in which we communicate beyond the words we speak.

Take control of your non-verbal signals

Messages and intentions are often misinterpreted because of our body language and non-verbal signals. We are all communicating all of the time, even when we are silent. As a manager, your team will be constantly watching you. They want to understand you and figure out what you're thinking. They'll be looking for clues in everything you say, but also in everything you do. When you are speaking, your actions and behaviours may contradict the words coming out of your mouth. When your mouth is closed, your body's still talking.

These non-verbal signals have been shown to have even more influence over what people think and believe than what is said. The tiniest behavioural signal that is misaligned with the topic, context or words can destroy your credibility as a leader and the trust others place in you. Whenever you find your message hasn't been heard in the way you had intended, it's likely your body language ruined it for you. By learning how to read the non-verbal signals of others, you can also understand whether your messages are being understood as you hope.

Non-verbal signals comprise more than just body language. Your behaviour also reveals a lot about you. Being unreliable and not honouring commitments tells people you don't regard them as important. Constantly arriving late for meetings tells people you consider your time more valuable than theirs. Not responding to an email when the sender expects a response tells them you're disorganized. Every action you take reveals something about your attitude and opinion, all of which is open to interpretation. It is not unusual for a team to have a completely false view of their manager just because they have mentally associated a few unrelated signals transmitted unintentionally.

What should you be conscious of to ensure your body sends out the same message as your mouth and mind? What are the non-verbal signals that are most likely to undermine the message we want to deliver?

Eye contact

Maintaining eye contact is an easy way to communicate interest, attention and confidence. Repeatedly looking away can be interpreted by others as a sign that you're uncomfortable in the situation, that you aren't fully sure of what you are talking about (since moving the eye to a neutral background is a way for the brain to divert energy to thinking), or that you're not interested in the person you're speaking with. When you're with someone, try to look them in the eyes both when you're speaking and when you're listening. You might find this awkward or uncomfortable to begin with, but people's impressions of you will improve if you do it.

Facial expressions

We speak with our faces, not just our mouths. Smiling, frowning, raising eyebrows – these can easily support or contradict what we say. Imagine how you would react if someone revealed some bad news or negative feedback while smiling, or how you would interpret positive news if delivered by a shifty or uninterested face.

Touching and fidgeting

Many people will subconsciously touch parts of their body, such as their mouth, neck or ears when they feel uncomfortable. Others may play with their pen (repeatedly clicking the nib in and out is one of the most annoying habits), twitch their leg or tap their fingers. These movements are interpreted as insecurity, immaturity and a lack of confidence. If you're prone to fidgeting, try interlocking your fingers and concentrating on maintaining that grip while in the presence of others.

Posture

Submissive people cross their legs and put their hands in their lap. Uninterested people slouch with their feet out in front of them. Hands in pockets conveys boredom and detachment. Instead, sit up straight, with your feet beneath your knees, and take command of the space around you. Mirroring the posture of the person you're speaking to is a highly effective way of building rapport. Leaning in creates the impression of interest in what someone is saying. Standing while presenting or speaking on the phone conveys authority and confidence.

Physical presentation

First impressions count for a lot. Your physical appearance is the first thing people will notice about you and it will guide their assumptions of who you are, your values, your seniority and your credibility before you've even begun speaking. Consider what signals your choice of clothes, hairstyle, jewellery, cosmetics and fragrance may send and whether these align with the image you want others to see.

....

Voice modulation

Your voice acts like a pipeline: it transfers your energy directly to your audience. A monotonous way of speaking – one that lacks variety in pace, volume or tone – will bore your audience, sap all engagement from the room and leave everyone wanting to disconnect from you. Your loudness, speed, modulation and intensity can all be used to support what you say – although bear in mind these can also be highly inappropriate if used in the wrong context (such as speaking loudly in a very sensitive or emotional situation).

....

Articulation

Strong articulation conveys credibility and enables comprehension. The use of gaps and pauses when you speak provides snippets of time to allow your audience to interpret and process what you have just said. The use of subconscious filler words, such as *um*, *er*, *you know* or *like* in place of silence makes it much harder for your audience to understand you, especially those whose native language is different from yours. They also make you sound immature and less intelligent.

Although body language is a tripwire waiting to topple you, it can also be harnessed to your advantage. Great leaders master body language to send subconscious signals to their audience that elevate their status. Often they are said to have 'presence'.

They bring with them an aura that can change the dynamics in a room as soon as they enter. In reality, their 'presence' is often simply derived from a mastery of their body language.

Become an active listener

Communication is not just about speaking; it also requires listening. How well we listen will determine how well we interpret what others are saying to us. Empathy is the ability to be in tune with the feelings and emotions of others. It allows you to understand what's not being said by the other person. A great way to develop your empathy is to become a more active listener, which requires listening to what others are really telling you through their words, tone, actions and body language.

Most people think they are good listeners. As with driving ability, the majority of people believe they are above average (which, of course, is mathematically impossible). Ask someone what listening is and they might tell you it is not talking when others are speaking. They might believe that *active* listening is signalling that you are actually listening through facial expressions like nodding and verbal sounds such as 'uh-huh'. In reality, most people are poor listeners for the simple reason that while someone else is speaking, they're mentally preparing what they will say next.

There are actually five levels of listening:

Avoidance listening
This is when you try to avoid listening to someone else by appearing preoccupied, distracted or uninterested. For example, if you don't want to break your concentration when someone comes over to your desk and begins

talking to you, you may nod and say 'uh-huh' without looking away from your screen.

....

Defensive listening

Each party listens purely to identify errors in the other side's logic or reasoning, creating a competitive environment where each just wants to outsmart the other. When the other side is speaking, you're preparing your next attack. By regarding the whole engagement through this defensive lens, you allow your emotions to cloud the facts and you'll be less likely to consider the points being made by the speaker.

....

Assumptive listening

This is when you listen but pay attention only to what you want or expect to hear. All you're interested in are comments that reaffirm your existing beliefs. This is very common in political discussions: each side is only interested in hearing viewpoints that align with how they already see the world.

....

Problem-solving listening

In this frame of mind, you listen in order to provide solutions. This is a typical question-and-answer conversation. It is a more lean-in exchange of information than the first three types of listening, but if the other person doesn't appreciate your ideas, they may feel patronized, misunderstood or resentful.

....

Active listening

This final type of listening is the only truly engaged form of listening that generates real rapport with someone. Here you listen in order to truly understand someone by discovering what's going on inside their head – what they are thinking, their emotional state, their fears and their ideas. While nodding may indicate you're listening, asking a probing question tells the speaker that you're also comprehending. With the first four forms of listening, you listen in order to share your opinion. With active listening, you listen to learn.

Becoming an active listener means consciously pushing yourself to achieve that fifth level of listening. To reach this level requires asking questions that encourage the speaker to open up a deeper level of information sharing. Active listening requires active questioning that builds on the speaker's previous answers. Most conversations can seem like a tennis match – the speaker's hat gets passed back and forth between one person and the other, each offering their own point of view on a topic. These conversations often don't build on what the other person has said. More effective conversations are like a soccer game, where each participant takes the ball a little further forward, building on the work of the other players, until eventually the ball gets close to the goal – the conclusion to the discussion. Here are some approaches that will help you become a more active listener:

Ask clarifying questions that promote discovery and insight

The best listeners are those who build on what has been said by asking questions that gently tease out more information or challenge assumptions in a constructive way. For example, 'How do you feel about that?' or 'Tell me more about that.'

Explicitly create a safe space for openness and honesty

Good listeners don't just contribute to the conversation; they make the conversation a positive experience for the other party. They ask questions and make comments that tell the other person they're in a safe space where issues and differences can be discussed openly. You can create a safe space through statements like 'I want to help' or 'I understand why you feel that way.'

Don't judge

The best conversations should lift someone up, not put them down. Assumptions can be challenged within active listening, but this should be done in a way that makes the listener feel they are being helped, not argued with. If you disagree with what the other person has said, comments like 'Could you look at this in a different way?' will encourage debate rather than rejection.

Read and act on the non-verbal signals

By listening out for what's not being said, you can peel away the superficial element of a conversation to uncover what's really going on in the other person's mind. By acknowledging when the non-verbals are telling a different story, a listener can form a much deeper connection with the speaker. If what you're seeing is different from what you're hearing, highlight this to get to the bottom of what the other party is really thinking. 'You look _____. Help me understand why.'

Keep the conversation about the other person

When you tell the other party that you've been in a similar situation, it seems like you're expressing empathy. In reality, all this does is make the conversion about you, not them. Your experiences and feelings may not be relevant to them. If they want your advice, they'll ask.

....

You may not need to say anything at all
The best listeners are those who do just that – listen. Someone who is in a high emotional state may simply be looking to let off steam. Having someone interrupt them isn't what they want. Sometimes it's best to say nothing at all.

There's a commonality across all these behaviours: an active listener contributes to the other person's train of thought instead of diverting from it. By clarifying, probing and supporting, you'll be able to take their ideas and amplify them, not just absorbing what they say but responding to it in a way that supports their thought process.

Beware the power of cognitive biases

No matter how actively we listen, our own subconscious assumptions can still misdirect our interpretation of what we have heard, creating conclusions that are not justified by the facts or evidence. Cognitive biases are the tendency for us to interpret information through our own past experiences and perceptions. We all do it and it's hard to escape from their grip. However, becoming more aware of them will make you less likely to fall prey to them.

There are six main biases that can misdirect our interpretations:

Confirmation bias
We all believe we're right and it's uncomfortable to contemplate that we might be wrong or have a misguided

opinion. Consequently, we tend to interpret new information in a way that confirms what we already think. Confirmation bias is at the heart of assumptive listening. We look for signals that reaffirm the views we already hold and ignore evidence that might contradict these. The most dangerous confirmation bias is that of the first impression. For example, if we see signals in the first few minutes of a job interview that cause us to like a candidate, we'll then spend the remainder of the interview subconsciously trying to confirm this opinion rather than testing for signs that the candidate may not be suitable after all.

Conservatism bias

Humans inherently dislike change and consequently we hold on to what we currently know and challenge opinions that are different. With conservatism bias, we are hesitant to support new evidence that contradicts old evidence and we push back on information that might cause us to discover we have been wrong about something in the past. Conservatism bias is at the heart of defensive listening.

Information bias

Sometimes we fail to make a decision because we don't trust our instincts and feel more data is needed. I'm a terrible shopper because I won't make a purchase decision until I have evaluated all possible options. Yet often I will end up buying the first item I looked at. Information bias is when you feel you need more data without appreciating whether the additional information will actually be useful or change the decision being considered.

Halo effect

We love predictability in our lives and we're pretty willing to believe that things are more consistent than they actually are. Life is easier that way as it requires less thinking about and less mental processing. If someone has done one thing well, we tend to assume they will be good at other things too. The halo effect is particularly prevalent among people who are physically attractive: because we like spending time in their company, we subconsciously assume they are also good at what they do.

Horns effect

This is the opposite of the halo effect. If our impressions about someone are negative, then we apply this lens to everything they do. If someone has done one thing badly, we assume they're useless and will be likely to underperform on something else, even if it's a completely different task.

Similarity bias

We naturally like people who are like us. We understand others better if they think, behave, look or dress the way we do. In recruitment this results in managers hiring people who have similar educational, cultural or experiential backgrounds to themselves. With the similarity bias, we're more likely to trust and believe people who seem like us. Similarity bias fuels subconscious racism and discrimination.

How do you prevent cognitive biases from infecting your conversations and tampering with the facts being presented? Your strongest defence is simply to be aware of them and recognize when one may have created a filter in your mind. If you like someone before they have revealed much about themselves, realize you've fallen for first-impression confirmation bias. If you've taken a dislike to someone, consciously look for reasons to like them. If someone has reacted emotionally to something you've said or done, prompt them to reconsider the facts, not their subconscious interpretation of them. If you've become upset or angry at someone else, remind yourself they probably didn't intend it. Become driven by facts, not assumptions or emotions. By employing active, connective listening techniques, you'll be better placed to avoid falling victim to cognitive biases.

How to make a great first impression

Your first meeting with the team you're going to manage will seem daunting, especially if you don't have an existing relationship with them. Your employees are likely to be as anxious as you. After all, their enjoyment of their jobs and ultimate contribution to the business are highly dependent upon them respecting you as their new boss and their perception as to whether you will be someone they will enjoy working for. Because human beings inherently dislike change, most people will subconsciously resist disrupting their current equilibrium, not because they disagree with the changes you might make but just because we all instinctively gravitate to the status quo. Your arrival will unsettle the team simply because their future is now more uncertain. They probably won't know what your plans are, how you like to manage or what your personality's like. If you have been brought in because the team's performance under the old regime was disappointing or relationships with your predecessor were broken, then some individuals might be thinking about resigning. Some will worry that you're going to make significant changes to their role. Others could have unrealistic expectations about how you're going to improve things. Everyone will already have formed opinions on whether your arrival will be good for them.

Confirmation bias can be your enemy here: everyone will be looking for proof that their assumptions about you and their future are correct. You can counter this by creating a great first impression that gives your team reasons to like you, respect your opinion and have a sense of optimism. So really think about what you say the first time you meet your team so you can allay their fears, prevent rumours from festering and outline a plan about what's going to happen next. The best thing you can do on your first day is provide reassurance and allow your employees to get to know you and your background, ideas and intentions as quickly as possible. Establishing your credibility and providing clarity will help put people at ease and go a long way to keeping the team motivated and engaged.

I've taken over many teams in my career and I have found that these are the kinds of questions your new employees will be seeking answers to:

- 'What have you achieved in your career to date that suggests you know what you're doing?' – Establish your credibility.

- 'What is your management style?' – Explain how you plan to run the team.

- 'How might things change in the way the team works or is structured?' – Explain your priorities for the team.

- 'How might my goals, objectives and day-to-day responsibilities change?' – Share your initial ideas on how you're going to improve things.

- 'Are you going to be a manager I can learn from, who will help me do well in my job and progress in my career?' – Outline how you plan to develop the team.

- 'Can I trust you?' – Establish yourself as an honest, transparent and trustworthy manager from the outset.

- 'How should I approach you with bad news?' – Emphasize the importance you place on creating a psychologically safe environment for everyone.

- 'Are you going to fit into the office dynamic and culture?' – Just be authentic.

I recommend you try to provide answers to most of these questions the first time you meet your team. Set yourself the goal that each employee will leave the office that evening excited about having you join their team and feeling positive about the future. First impressions matter and they are hard to repair once people have formed negative assumptions about you. Laying out your stall to explain how you plan to operate will demonstrate your own self-awareness and grasp of the job, and show that you plan to help them to succeed both as individuals and as a team.

Let people know that you'll be scheduling one-to-one meetings with each of them over the following few days in which they will be able to ask you further questions. Use these meetings to get to know them, their fears, aspirations and ideas for change. In addition to discovering what each person does in their role, your questions should deepen your understanding of each individual's unique history, skills, experience and personality so that you can begin to tailor your interactions and communications. Being attentive to each person as an individual – their engagement, interests and ambitions – may forestall any impending resignations or reservations.

Open questions are an excellent way of uncovering fresh ideas and hidden issues. Here are ten suggestions you can use during these early one-to-one meetings to help encourage your employees to open up to you:

- 'Tell me about yourself. How have you got to where you are now?'

- 'What do you like about your job? Describe a good day.'

- 'What don't you like about your job? Describe a bad day.'

- 'Do you feel your skills are being used to the fullest? What would you like to do more of? What would you want to do less of?'

- 'What isn't working properly in the team? What's getting in your way of achieving the best results? What would you suggest we do differently?'

- 'How would you describe the current culture in the team? What do you like about it? What would you change?'

- 'What would you like to do after this role? When do you think you'll be ready for a change? What's standing in your way of getting there?'

- 'How would you like us to work together? How can I best support you to deliver great work?'

- 'How do you like to receive feedback?'

- 'What are the top three things you think I should focus on?'

Finally, at the end of each one-to-one meeting with your new team, send the employee off on a wave of optimism by reinforcing how excited you are about working with them, how committed you are to ensuring they are successful and happy in their job, and how you'll be relying upon them to continue to deliver great work. Sharing something personal with them, such as highlighting a common educational background or sporting interest, or flattering them with comments on the great things you've already heard about them, is an easy way to build likeability.

Chapter takeaways

- Effective listening and communicating will underpin everything you do as a manager, and can make or break your career.

- Communication happens when the message you send is heard, interpreted and actioned as you expect. Misunderstandings occur when the message that's received is different from the one you intended to send because other signals, such as tone or body language, seeded doubt or confusion.

- Non-verbal signals carry more weight than the words you say and are the greatest cause of miscommunication. Become conscious of the habits and behaviours you exhibit in the presence of others that might undermine their trust and confidence in what you say.

- Truly active listening is when you listen to learn, not to comment. It requires you to build on what the other person has said rather than just present your own perspective on it.

- We all have cognitive biases, which act as lenses through which we see the world. Become aware of when they are misleading you by causing you to assume something that isn't borne out by the facts and try to spot when others have succumbed to them.

- Make a great first impression by providing clarity about who you are, your view of the team and its goals and what you do or don't plan to change.

Part 3: Becoming the Manager You Aspire to Be

Putting Theory into Practice

Commit to an experiential learning experience

You should now have a broad understanding of the expectations that your team will place on you as their manager and what you can do to extract the best performance from them. In Part 2 we covered the five pillars of my people management framework and explained how you can use each to become a great manager who is able to drive superior performance from your employees. To recap, they are:

1 Motivation.

2 Expectations.

3 Development.

4 Culture.

5 Communication.

Your growth into a highly effective, respected and valued manager began when you started reading this book, but it won't end when you put it down. Managing people is a continuous learning experience. You'll only become a great manager by implementing the theories and best practices we've covered. Constantly forcing yourself to behave in ways that are different from what may be natural for you will prove exhausting, both physically and mentally. Be prepared for this and accept it. While there's so much you'll need to think about, small changes made on a daily basis will multiply into massive improvements over time. Habits are formed through regular repetition. By making a commitment to yourself to do a few things differently each month, and focusing on doing those things consistently for that month, you'll gain practical experience and turn those behaviours into habits so that they become the way you instinctively operate.

You may feel daunted and overwhelmed by the long list of things you'll need to think about – especially as you're likely to have other operational responsibilities too. If you've reached this point in the book with a sense of fear, trepidation, anxiousness or self-doubt around the sheer number of things that you'll need to get right to become an effective manager, then you may now be wondering whether you're even capable of living up to the expectations I've laid out. Becoming a manager can be terrifying. It's likely to require a huge emotional and psychological adjustment. Your personality will come under the spotlight, others will judge everything you do and say, your decisions will have consequences far beyond your own work and the misinterpretation of careless body language that was previously inconsequential will now have the potential for creating huge repercussions. But managing other people can also be immensely rewarding. Leading a team of highly capable, motivated and energized individuals is a huge privilege. The satisfaction you'll get from seeing them succeed and become recognized as leading a high-performing team is immense. Your team will remember you for life and you'll never forget an exceptional team you've had the privilege of leading.

While there's lots you will need to master to become a world-class manager, you can still be highly effective by doing a limited set of tasks really well. To make things easy for you, here are the twenty most important things you should focus on. Get these right and you'll be well down your path to becoming an awesome manager who's loved by your employees and able to deliver astonishing results.

The 20 most important things to get right

Motivate your employees

1 Discover what each employee actually enjoys doing.

2 Identify each employee's strengths and figure out how to harness these in the best ways.

3 Continually emphasize why each person's job matters.

4 Establish clear expectations for every team member and track progress regularly.

5 Give clear direction when delegating and provide people with autonomy.

6 Deal with complaints about compensation to prevent these from smothering all other motivations.

7 Address any disengagement before it poisons the whole team.

Provide feedback and coaching

8 Provide regular, honest and direct feedback.

9 Give five pieces of praise for every one piece of developmental feedback.

10 Set high expectations and deal with underperformance quickly and visibly to reinforce these standards.

11 Ask for feedback from your team about how well you're supporting them.

Create the optimal environment for high performance

12 Establish a collective feeling of psychological safety in your group.

13 Create and maintain transparency and trust between you and each employee.

14 Deal with unwanted behaviours immediately, especially when group norms are threatened.

15 Remove all barriers to productive work, such as ineffective technology, unnecessary bureaucracy, time-wasting meetings and inefficient processes.

Be personally effective

16 Build strong informal authority by investing in relationships with others and showing you are reliable, trustworthy, organized and capable.

17 Make quick, clear decisions and seek everyone's acceptance of these, even if they don't agree with them.

18 Show genuine interest in each team member beyond the work they do.

19 Communicate with confidence and clarity, and be conscious of your body language.

20 Always remember that your team doesn't work for you – you work for them.

Finally, don't forget that you are an employee to another manager somewhere. Even if you're an entrepreneur or CEO, you'll probably have shareholders you'll answer to. Now that you have some insight into how to manage your own team, think about how you could work more effectively with your own manager. They will be dealing with the same challenges as you. They can be a source of support and advice for you when things go wrong, as well as a cause of stress and anxiety if they don't work with you in the ways you want. Reading this book should have left you well prepared to engage in a frank conversation with your own manager to explore how you could both work together more effectively. Why not arrange one today?

Being a manager who is recognized for bringing the best out of their team is an immensely rewarding job. Your team will appreciate your guidance and support, you'll deliver real impact for your organization and you'll build lasting personal relationships that make going to work every day so much more enjoyable. Put in the effort to continually improve by following the guidance I have shared in this book and you'll be rewarded with personal satisfaction and an accelerated career trajectory. Your legacy will be a group of individuals who will go on to achieve amazing things in their own careers because of your encouragement, support and guidance.

Good luck and enjoy the journey.

Access more resources and ideas to support you at www.managingpeople.tips

Notes

Introduction

1 William Gentry, *Be the Boss Everyone Wants to Work for: A Guide for New Leaders* (Berrett-Koehler, 2016).

2 'New DDI Research: 57 Percent of Employees Quit Because of Their Boss', DDI Frontline Leader Project press release, 9 December 2019; www.prnewswire.com/news-releases/new-ddi-research-57-percent-of-employees-quit-because-of-their-boss-300971506.html.

3 Heather R. Huhman, 'Research Shows That Your First-Time Managers Aren't Ready to Lead', Entrepreneur.com, 19 February 2018; www.entrepreneur.com/article/309052.

4 'More Than One-Quarter of Managers Said They Weren't Ready to Lead', CareerBuilder Survey, 28 March 2011; http://press.careerbuilder.com/2011-03-28-More-Than-One-Quarter-of-Managers-Said-They-Werent-Ready-to-Lead-When-They-Began-Managing-Others-Finds-New-CareerBuilder-Survey. 'New Managers Aren't Getting the Training They Need to Succeed', Ken Blanchard Companies, 9 October 2016; https://leadingwithtrust.com/2016/10/09/infographic-new-managers-arent-getting-the-training-they-need-to-succeed/.

Why Being a Great Manager Matters

1 Glassdoor, 'New Research Finds That Higher Employee Satisfaction Improves UK Company Financial Performance', 29 March 2018 https://about-content.glassdor.com/en-us/new-research-finds-that-higher-employee-satisfaction-improves-uk-company-financial-performance.

2　Clement S. Bellet, Jan-Emmanuel de Neve and George Ward, 'Does Employee Happiness Have an Impact on Productivity', Saïd Business School WP 2019-13, University of Oxford, October 2019; http://dx.doi.org/10.2139/ssrn.3470734.

3　Margaret Ousby, 'UK Productivity Slowdown Unprecedented in 250 Years – New Study Shows', University of Sussex; www.sussex.ac.uk/broadcast/read/51253.

4　Gallup, *State of the Global Workplace, 2020*; www.gallup.com/workplace/238079/state-global-workplace-2020.aspx.

5　Michelle Toh and Yoko Wakatsuki, 'Microsoft tried a 4-day workweek in Japan. Productivity jumped 40%', *CNN Business*, 18 November 2019; https://edition.cnn.com/2019/11/04/tech/microsoft-japan-workweek-productivity/index.html.

6　'The Perpetual Guardian Four-Day Week Trial', 4dayweek.com; https://4dayweek.com/four-day-week-trial.

7　David Sturt and Todd Nordstrom, '10 Shocking Workplace Stats You Need To Know', *Forbes*, 8 March 2018; www.forbes.com/sites/davidsturt/2018/03/08/10-shocking-workplace-stats-you-need-to-know.

8　Leslie Brokaw, 'How to Be a Better Boss', *MIT Sloan Management Review*, 4 December 2013; https://sloanreview.mit.edu/article/how-to-be-a-better-boss/.

The Bad Habits You Must Break

1　'New DDI Research: 57 Percent of Employees Quit Because of Their Boss', DDI Frontline Leader Project press release, 9 December 2019; www.prnewswire.com/news-releases/new-ddi-research-57-percent-of-employees-quit-because-of-their-boss-300971506.html.

2　Research results from Project Oxygen, Google, 2008 onwards; https://rework.withgoogle.com/blog/the-evolution-of-project-oxygen/.

3　Jeff Miller, 'More than Half of New Managers Fail: Here's How to Avoid Their Common Mistakes', Inc.com, 19 September 2017; www.inc.com/jeff-miller/more-than-half-of-new-managers-fail-heres-how-to-a.html.

4　Liz Wiseman, *Multipliers: How the Best Leaders Make Everyone Smarter* (HarperBusiness, 2010).

What Your Employees Need from You

1   Research results from Project Oxygen, Google, 2008 onwards; https://rework.withgoogle.com/blog/the-evolution-of-project-oxygen/.

Step 1: Activate Motivation

1   Dr Mary Hayes et al., 'The Global Study of Engagement Technical Report', ADP Research Institute, 2019; www.adp.com/-/media/adp/ResourceHub/pdf/ADPRI/ADPRI0102_2018_Engagement_Study_Technical_Report_RELEASE%20READY.ashx.

2   William Samuelson and Richard Zeckhauser, 'Status Quo Bias in Decision Making', *Journal of Risk and Uncertainty*, 1(1), March 1988, 7–59.

3   Sonali Basak, 'Dimon Goes to War on JPMorgan Bureaucracy', *Bloomberg Business*, 5 April 2018, www.bloomberg.com/news/articles/2018-04-05/dimon-goes-to-war-on-jpmorgan-bureaucracy-isn-t-hot-on-meetings.

4   *Guardian*, 13 January 2021.

5   Staples, *Workplace Survey, 2019*; www.staples.com/content-hub/productivity/workplace-strategy/staples-workplace-survey-2019.

6   Ed Catmull, *Creativity, Inc.: Overcoming the Unseen Forces That Stand in the Way of True Inspiration* (Bantam Press, 2014), p. 109.

7   Mihàly Csìkszentmihàlyi, *Flow: The Psychology of Optimal Experience* (HarperPerennial, 2008).

8   Margaret M. Luciano and Joan F. Brett, 'Do You Know Burnout When You See It?', *Harvard Business Review*, 28 January 2021; https://hbr.org/2021/01/do-you-know-burnout-when-you-see-it. Jennifer Moss, 'Burnout is About Your Workplace, Not Your People', *Harvard Business Review*, 11 December 2019; https://hbr.org/2019/12/burnout-is-about-your-workplace-not-your-people.

9   Roland G. Fryer Jr et al., 'Enhancing the Efficacy of Teacher Incentives Through Loss Aversion: A Field Experiment', NBER Working Paper 18237, July 2012; www.nber.org/papers/w18237.

Step 2: Define and Track Expectations

1 Deloitte, 'Global Human Capital Trends 2014: Engaging the 21st-Century Workforce'; https://documents.deloitte.com/insights/HCTrends2014.

2 Corporate Leadership Council, *Building the High-Performance Workforce: A Quantitative Analysis of the Effectiveness of Performance Management Strategies* (Corporate Executive Board, 2002).

Step 4: Build a High-Performance Culture

1 Charles Duhigg, 'What Google Learned from Its Quest to Build the Perfect Team', *New York Times*, 25 February 2016; www.nytimes.com/2016/02/28/magazine/what-google-learned-from-its-quest-to-build-the-perfect-team.html.

2 Susie Cranston and Scott Keller, 'Increasing the "Meaning Quotient" of Work', *McKinsey Quarterly*, January 2013; www.mckinsey.com/business-functions/organization/our-insights/increasing-the-meaning-quotient-of-work.

3 Justin Bariso, 'Elon Musk and Jeff Bezos Just Dropped the Best Business Advice You'll Read Today', Inc.com, 26 April 2018; www.inc.com/justin-bariso/jeff-bezos-elon-musk-just-taught-a-master-class-in-how-to-run-a-company.html. Justin Bariso, 'In Just 3 Words, Amazon's Jeff Bezos Taught a Brilliant Lesson in Leadership', Inc.com, 13 April 2017; www.inc.com/justin-bariso/it-took-jeff-bezos-only-three-words-to-drop-the-best-advice-youll-hear-today.html.

Further Reading

Introduction

William Gentry, *Be the Boss Everyone Wants to Work for: A Guide for New Leaders* (Berrett-Koehler, 2016)

Heather R. Huhman, 'Research Shows That Your First-Time Managers Aren't Ready to Lead', Entrepreneur.com, 19 February 2018; www.entrepreneur.com/article/309052

Why Being a Great Manager Matters

Clement S. Bellet, Jan-Emmanuel de Neve and George Ward, 'Does Employee Happiness Have an Impact on Productivity', Saïd Business School WP 2019-13, University of Oxford, October 2019; http://dx.doi.org/10.2139/ssrn.3470734

Julian Birkinshaw, *Becoming a Better Boss: Why Good Management is So Difficult* (Jossey-Bass, 2013)

Julian Birkinshaw and Jonas Ridderstråle, *Fast/Forward: Make Your Company Fit for the Future* (Stanford Business Books, 2017)

Della Bradshaw, 'Do the Financial Benefits of an MBA Outweigh the Costs?', *Financial Times*, 29 January 2017; www.ft.com/content/e77b50ba-d9b1-11e6-944b-e7eb37a6aa8e

Andrew Chamberlain, 'Does Company Culture Pay Off?', Glassdoor, March 2015, www.glassdoor.com/research/app/uploads/sites/2/2015/03/GD_Report_1-1.pdf

4 day week, 'The Perpetual Guardian Four-Day Week Trial', 4dayweek.com; https://4dayweek.com/four-day-week-trial.

Neil Franklin, 'Nearly Half of Employees Worldwide Could Do Their Jobs in 5 Hours or Fewer Each Day', Workplace Insight, September

2014; https://workplaceinsight.net/nearly-half-of-employees-worldwide-could-do-their-jobs-in-5-hours-or-less-each-day/

William Gentry, *Be the Boss Everyone Wants to Work for: A Guide for New Leaders* (Berrett-Koehler, 2016)

T. Clifton Green, Ruoyan Huang, Quan Wen and Dexin Xhou, 'Crowdsourced Employer Reviews and Stock Returns', *Journal of Financial Economics* 134(1), October 2019, 236–51

Minjie Huang, Pingshu Li, Felix Meschke, James P. Guthrie, 'Family Firms, Employee Satisfaction, and Corporate Performance', *Journal of Corporate Finance* 34, October 2015, 108–27

Efthymia Symitsi, Panagiotis Stamolampros, George Daskalakis and Nikolaos Korfiatic, 'Employee Satisfaction and Corporate Performance in the UK', SSRN Electronic Journal, 10.2139/ssrn.3140512, February 2018

VoucherCloud, 'How Many Productive Hours in a Workday?'; www.vouchercloud.com/resources/office-worker-productivity

Liz Wiseman, *Multipliers: How the Best Leaders Make Everyone Smarter* (HarperBusiness, 2010)

The Bad Habits You Must Break

Jeff Miller, 'More than Half of New Managers Fail: Here's How to Avoid Their Common Mistakes', Inc.com, 19 September 2017; www.inc.com/jeff-miller/more-than-half-of-new-managers-fail-heres-how-to-a.html

Liz Wiseman, *Multipliers: How the Best Leaders Make Everyone Smarter* (HarperBusiness, 2010)

What Your Employees Need from You

Julian Birkinshaw, *Becoming a Better Boss: Why Good Management is So Difficult* (Jossey-Bass, 2013)

Melissa Harrell and Lauren Barbato, 'Great Managers Still Matter: The Evolution of Google's Project Oxygen', Google, February 2018; https://rework.withgoogle.com/blog/the-evolution-of-project-oxygen/

Michael Schneider, 'Google Employees Weighed in on What Makes a Highly Effective Manager', Inc.com, 20 June 2017; www.inc.com/

michael-schneider/google-did-an-internal-study-that-will-forever-change-how-they-hire-and-promote-.html

Liz Wiseman, *Multipliers: How the Best Leaders Make Everyone Smarter* (HarperBusiness, 2010)

Step 1: Activate Motivation

Julian Birkinshaw, 'New Ways of Working: Getting Beyond Bureaucracy', *Forbes*, 7 November 2019; www.forbes.com/sites/lbsbusinessstrategyreview/2019/11/07/new-ways-of-working-getting-beyond-bureaucracy/?sh=4cd29c137a84

George Bradt, 'The Keys to Level Four Delegation – The Heart of Leadership', *Forbes*, 10 September 2019; www.forbes.com/sites/georgebradt/2019/09/10/the-keys-to-level-four-delegation--the-heart-of-leadership/?sh=6b5add082c28

Paul Frampton Calero, '4 Reasons Why We Need to Reimagine Work', Linkedin, August 2019; www.linkedin.com/pulse/future-work-overdue-some-distant-time-years-from-now-frampton-calero

Susie Cranston and Scott Keller, 'Increasing the "Meaning Quotient" of Work', *McKinsey Quarterly*, January 2013; www.mckinsey.com/business-functions/organization/our-insights/increasing-the-meaning-quotient-of-work#

Edward Deci and Richard M. Ryan, *Intrinsic Motivation and Self-Determination in Human Behaviour* (Springer US, 1985)

Neil Franklin, 'Nearly Half of Employees Worldwide Could Do Their Jobs in 5 Hours or Fewer Each Day', Workplace Insight, September 2014; https://workplaceinsight.net/nearly-half-of-employees-worldwide-could-do-their-jobs-in-5-hours-or-less-each-day

Ben Hunt-Davis, *Will It Make The Boat Go Faster? Olympic-winning Strategies for Everyday Success* (Troubador Publishing, 2011)

Caterina Kostoula, '13 Free Ways to Motivate Your Employees Right Now', The Leaderpath; www.theleaderpath.com

Margaret M. Luciano and Joan F. Brett, 'Do You Know Burnout When You See It?', *Harvard Business Review*, 28 January 2021; https://hbr.org/2021/01/do-you-know-burnout-when-you-see-it

Lindsay McGregor and Neel Doshi, 'How Company Culture Shapes

Employee Motivation', *Harvard Business Review*, 25 November 2015; https://hbr.org/2015/11/how-company-culture-shapes-employee-motivation

MindTools, 'Herzberg's Motivators and Hygiene Factors', www.mindtools.com/pages/article/herzberg-motivators-hygiene-factors.htm

Jennifer Moss, 'Burnout is About Your Workplace, Not Your People', *Harvard Business Review*, 11 December 2019; https://hbr.org/2019/12/burnout-is-about-your-workplace-not-your-people

Daniel Pink, *Drive: The Surprising Truth About What Motivates Us* (Riverhead Books, 2011)

Tony Schwartz, 'Create a Growth Culture, Not a Performance-Obsessed One', *Harvard Business Review*, 7 March 2018; https://hbr.org/2018/03/create-a-growth-culture-not-a-performance-obsessed-one

Staples, *Workplace Survey, 2019*; https://marketingassets.staples.com/m/5644f1362b2dfad2/original/Staples-Workplace-Survey-2019.pdf

Brad Stulberg and Steve Magness, *The Passion Paradox: A Guide to Going All in, Finding Success, and Discovering the Benefits of an Unbalanced Life* (Rodale Books, 2019)

Patrick Wong, 'Does More Money Change What We Value At Work?', Glassdoor, January 2017; www.glassdoor.com/research/more-money-change-value-at-work/#

Step 2: Define and Track Expectations

Marcus Buckingham and Ashley Goodall, 'Reinventing Performance Management', *Harvard Business Review*, April 2015; https://hbr.org/2015/04/reinventing-performance-management

Dick Grote, *How to Be Good at Performance Appraisals: Simple, Effective, Done Right* (Harvard Business Press, 2011)

Edwin A. Locke and Gary P. Latham, 'Building a Practically Useful Theory of Goal Setting and Task Motivation: A 35-Year Odyssey', *American Psychologist* 57(9), 2002, 705–17

Steven E. Scullen, Michael K. Mount and Maynard Goff, 'Understanding the Latent Structure of Job Performance Ratings', *Journal of Applied Psychology* 85(6), 2000, 956–70

Christina R. Wodtke, *Radical Focus: Achieving Your Most Important Goals with Objectives and Key Results* (Cucina Media, 2016)

Step 3: Develop Your Employees

Alison Wood Brooks, Francesca Gino and Maurice E. Schweitzer, 'Smart People Ask for My Advice: Seeking Advice Boosts Perceptions of Confidence', *Management Science* 61(6), 2015; https://doi.org/10.1287/mnsc.2014.2054

Elle Caplan, '8 Things Exceptional Bosses Constantly Tell Their Employees', Inc.com; www.inc.com/elle-kaplan/8-things-exceptional-bosses-constantly-tell-their-employees.html

Corporate Executive Board (now Gartner), *Head of L&D Manager Effectiveness Survey*, 2017

First Round Review, 'How to Be a Career Changing Mentor', https://firstround.com/review/how-to-be-a-career-changing-mentor-25-tips-from-the-best-mentors-we-know

Jeff Haden, 'How Great Bosses Motivate Employees? The Best Answer Ever', Inc.com; www.inc.com/jeff-haden/how-to-motivate-employees-the-best-answer-ever.html

Alan Matthews, *How to Design and Deliver Great Training* (HLS Publishing Solutions, 2012)

Melanie Moorcroft and Mary Ann Crick, *A Guide to Mentoring*, People and Organisational Development, University of Auckland, 2014; https://cdn.auckland.ac.nz/assets/auckland/business/current-students/PDFs/mentoring-guide-final.pdf

Marcel Schwantes, 'Here's How Good Managers Give Bad Employees Feedback', Inc.com; www.inc.com/marcel-schwantes/heres-how-good-managers-give-bad-employees-feedback.html

———, '10 Magic Phrases You Need to Say Often to Increase Trust', Inc.com; www.inc.com/marcel-schwantes/10-magic-phrases-you-need-to-say-often-to-increase-trust.html

Step 4: Build a High-Performance Culture

Justin Bariso, 'Elon Musk and Jeff Bezos Just Dropped the Best Business Advice You'll Read Today', Inc.com, 26 April 2018; www.inc.com/justin-bariso/jeff-bezos-elon-musk-just-taught-a-master-class-in-how-to-run-a-company.html

———, 'In Just 3 Words, Amazon's Jeff Bezos Taught a Brilliant Lesson in Leadership', Inc.com, 13 April 2017; www.inc.com/justin-bariso/

it-took-jeff-bezos-only-three-words-to-drop-the-best-advice-youll-hear-today.html

Susie Cranston and Scott Keller, 'Increasing the "Meaning Quotient" of Work', *McKinsey Quarterly*, January 2013; www.mckinsey.com/business-functions/organization/our-insights/increasing-the-meaning-quotient-of-work

Nancy Duarte, 'Good Leadership is About Communicating "Why"', *Harvard Business Review*, 6 May 2020; https://hbr.org/2020/05/good-leadership-is-about-communicating-why

Charles Duhigg, 'What Google Learned from Its Quest to Build the Perfect Team', *New York Times*, 25 February 2016; www.nytimes.com/2016/02/28/magazine/what-google-learned-from-its-quest-to-build-the-perfect-team.html

First Round Review, 'Struggling to Thrive as a Large Team Working Remotely? This Exec Has the Field Guide You Need'; https://firstround.com/review/struggling-to-thrive-as-a-large-team-working-remotely-this-exec-has-the-field-guide-you-need/

Forbes Coaches Council, '14 Warning Signs That Your Team is Nearing Dysfunction', *Forbes*, 26 August 2016; www.forbes.com/sites/forbescoachescouncil/2016/08/26/14-warning-signs-that-your-team-is-nearing-dysfunction

Barbara L. Fredrickson, 'Positive Emotions Broaden and Build', University of North Carolina at Chapel Hill, 2013; https://peplab.web.unc.edu/wp-content/uploads/sites/18901/2019/06/Fredrickson2013ChapteronBnBinAESP.pdf

Jennifer Moss, 'Burnout Is About Your Workplace, Not Your People', *Harvard Business Review*, 11 December 2019; https://hbr.org/2019/12/burnout-is-about-your-workplace-not-your-people

Step 5: Master Your Communication

Mark Goulston and John Ullmen, 'Are You Listening?', American Management Association, 24 January 2019; www.amanet.org/articles/are-you-listening-/

Judith Humphrey, 'These Emotionally Intelligent Habits Can Make You a Better Listener', *Fast Company*, 9 November 2017;

www.fastcompany.com/40493058/these-emotionally-
intelligent-habits-can-make-you-a-better-listener

Jack Zenger and Joseph Folkman, 'What Great Listeners Actually Do',
Harvard Business Review, 14 July 2016; https://hbr.org/2016/07/
what-great-listeners-actually-do

Acknowledgements

I was inspired to write this book by the countless stories of terrible management practices my friends, family, colleagues and acquaintances have shared with me over the last twenty years. It would betray their confidence, as well as be impractical, to name everyone who shared their personal experience or anecdote with me, but I'd like to express my thanks to all those who trusted me as a sympathetic recipient of their plight.

I've crafted my own management skills through the many teams I've had the privilege of leading over the years. Thank you to everyone from my teams at International Volunteer HQ, KPEX, L2, Axonix, Telefónica, Google, 3M and Proximity London for accompanying me on this journey and providing me with opportunities to test and practise the approaches I've subsequently summarized in this book. Your honest feedback was of enormous help in my own self-development, especially when I didn't get things right.

One of those employees, Caterina Kostoula, introduced me to Penguin, so I owe a special expression of gratitude to her. My team at International Volunteer HQ kindly agreed to sit through my first interation of this book as a training course; the questions they asked and feedback they gave proved invaluable in helping me to improve the book's structure and content. Thank you to all those who persisted through each module.

Thank you also to my other friends who provided me with feedback on early drafts.

The editing team at Penguin gave me superb feedback and really helped me to polish my narrative, so thank you Celia Buzuk, Ellie Smith and Trevor Horwood in particular.

Finally, my husband Christopher has been an invaluable source of inspiration, guidance, best practices and bad management case studies through his own career and research in this area. He's also been a wise and perceptive editor as I worked through initial ideas and early drafts. Thank you for being an extremely patient and supportive partner, and for reading this book so many times.

Index

PENGUIN PARTNERSHIPS

Penguin Partnerships is the Creative Sales and Promotions team at Penguin Random House. We have a long history of working with clients on a wide variety of briefs, specializing in brand promotions, bespoke publishing and retail exclusives, plus corporate, entertainment and media partnerships.

We can respond quickly to briefs and specialize in repurposing books and content for sales promotions, for use as incentives and retail exclusives as well as creating content for new books in collaboration with our partners as part of branded book relationships.

Equally if you'd simply like to buy a bulk quantity of one of our existing books at a special discount, we can help with that too. Our books can make excellent corporate or employee gifts.

Special editions, including personalized covers, excerpts of existing books or books with corporate logos can be created in large quantities for special needs.

We can work within your budget to deliver whatever you want, however you want it.

For more information, please contact
salesenquiries@penguinrandomhouse.co.uk